"Whom have you got on board?" said I. Said he, "Astrologers, fortune-tellers, alchymists, rhymers, poets, painters, projectors, mathematicians, watch-makers, sing-songs, musicianers, and the devil and all of others that are subject to Queen Whims. They have very fair legible patents to show for it, as anybody may see." Panurge had no sooner heard this, but he was upon the high-rope, and began to rail at them like mad.

The Heroic Deeds of Gargantua and Pantagruel

FRANÇOIS RABELAIS

BENJAMIN B. KING

NOTES ON
THE MECHANICS
OF
GROWTH AND DEBT

Distributed by The Johns Hopkins Press
Baltimore, Maryland

FOREWORD

I would like to explain *why* the World Bank Group does research work, and why it publishes it. We feel an obligation to look beyond the projects we help to finance towards the whole resource allocation of an economy, and the effectiveness of the use of those resources. Our major concern, in dealings with member countries, is that all scarce resources, including capital, skilled labor, enterprise and know-how, should be used to their best advantage. We want to see policies that encourage appropriate increases in the supply of savings, whether domestic or international. Finally, we are required by our Articles, as well as by inclination, to use objective economic criteria in all our judgments.

These are our preoccupations, and these, one way or another, are the subjects of most of our research work. Clearly, they are also the proper concerns of anyone who is interested in promoting development, and so we seek to make our research papers widely available. In doing so, we have to take the risk of being misunderstood. Although these studies are published by the Bank, the views expressed and the methods explored should not necessarily be considered to represent the Bank's views or policies. Rather they are offered as a modest contribution to the great discussion on how to advance the economic development of the underdeveloped world.

ROBERT S. McNAMARA
President
International Bank for Reconstruction and Development

August 15, 1968

TABLE OF CONTENTS

Notation
— nil or negligible
... not available

PREFACE

Every bank is interested in the debt servicing capacity of its clients. It is not surprising therefore that international debt and its burden on nations is a traditional subject of study for economists in the Bank. This paper originated as a comment on some conclusions in the longer-term analysis in *Economic Growth and External Debt* (1964), and thus represents a continuation of that discussion. There is every prospect that the relations between growth and debt, once a peculiar concern of planners and of public lenders, will attract wider attention in the future, as the realities of "the long haul" in development become explicit. That is why we are opening to the public what might otherwise be thought of as a private debate.

Cournot in his *Souvenirs* over a hundred years ago wrote that the function of prediction is not to foretell the future but to cast a sharper light on the present. I suggest that the wise use of the ideas presented in B. B. King's *Notes* will help us to analyze better the present debt position of many countries.

ANDREW M. KAMARCK
Director,
Economics Department

AUTHOR'S NOTE

The author is indebted to Bela Balassa for many pertinent comments and for patient encouragement at every stage. Other useful comments came from Hugh Collier at an earlier stage and from Ted Hawkins, Nicholas Carter, and Atle Elsaas in the later ones. Huguette Angel wrote the program for the tables on the accumulation function; the numerical examples were checked by Constantinos Giatrakos and Rogelio David; Germaine Gagnon typed the manuscript indefatigably. The editor, Hugh Latimer, has been more than helpful throughout in a variety of ways. No one but the author is responsible for any mistakes.

B. B. K.

I

INTRODUCTION

This paper grew out of an exploration of the way in which inflow of capital from abroad affects the growth of an economy, if there is a return flow of interest payments on the debt thereby created. There are two sides to this coin. The obverse is to suppose that the creditor country or countries supplies a given amount of capital on certain terms; what then happens to the growth of the recipient country? The reverse is to set a target rate of growth for the recipient country; what then is required of the donor countries in the way of aid to the recipient country? Models which answer some of these questions, on certain assumptions, exist already of course.[1] The answer will be different according to the dominant constraints on the economy, i.e. whether there is a balance of payments or a savings gap. In this paper we shall only be concerned with the savings gap, not out of a conviction that the other gap can be ignored, but only because there is an advantage in taking one thing at a time.

Most such models end up with rather long mathematical expres-

---

[1] For example, H. B. Chenery and A. M. Strout, "Foreign Assistance and Economic Development," *American Economic Review*, LVI, Number 4, Part 1 (September 1966); Dragoslav Avramovic and Associates, *Economic Growth and External Debt*, (Johns Hopkins Press, Baltimore 1964).

sions, whether they are in exponential form or in compound interest form. This is of course not very surprising. Growth, if one assumes a constant rate, introduces one element of compound interest. The interest on the debt itself introduces another. If one supposes that the inflow of capital is the generating factor, and that it is increasing at a particular rate, then one has a third rate of growth to contend with.

An unexpected by-product of the exploration is a mathematical function which has here been called the accumulation function. It has been given this name because the expressions which give rise to it are a result of accumulation in one form or another at compound interest or a kind of compound compound interest. With the aid of it, it is possible to reduce the long mathematical expressions to a simple notation. Furthermore, it is possible to work with this function in a reasonably simple way.

The function is in fact only an extension of the sort of expressions that one finds in annuity tables. But instead of one rate of growth there may be two or three. Since this function, which is introduced in Chapter II, is new, it imposes a burden on the reader, even though most of the more esoteric mathematics have been relegated to Annex 1. Those who have no stomach for such things had better stop at this point. But those who feel inclined to try to master it—it is not that difficult—may find that it has wider application than growth or debt models.

Now it is one thing to build up these long mathematical expressions in a model, insert specific figures in the place of the symbols and then to make statements about the results. It is another thing to understand why, when one changes the values of the parameters, certain things happen. Do they happen because of some inviolable law of nature or do they happen because some implicit assumption has been built into the model? It is not usually easy to give an answer to this question as long as the model is in a rather complicated form.

A second result of this exploration into the construction of a model is the finding that it makes a good deal of difference whether one uses a marginal domestic savings concept or a marginal national savings concept. That there should be a difference is of course not at all surprising. Although to any national savings rate at any given time there is obviously a corresponding domestic savings rate, there can be no such thing as identity over time if the relationship between investment income and gross domestic product is changing. To assume that savings according to one concept are constant is to assume that savings according to the other are not; and vice versa.

But the difference goes further than that. The concept of a domestic savings rate in itself implies that any increment in investment income flowing out of the country concerned automatically reduces savings available for investment by exactly the same amount. On this questionable hypothesis, it is perfectly easy to conceive of a case where an inflow of capital from abroad can retard the growth of an economy rather than advance it. This can lead to the *reductio ad absurdum* that, given enough external aid, GDP will be reduced to zero.

The concept of a national savings rate, however, implies that only a portion of an increment in investment income will be subtracted from the savings available for investment. Under any ordinary circumstances, it is virtually impossible to conceive of a case where an inflow of capital could retard the growth of the economy. There is, therefore, a question which is right. While there is a case to be made for supposing that savings are, in some sense, a function of disposable income (i.e. after deduction of investment income going abroad), it is quite possible that neither is right but that the truth may lie between, and the answer how far between may differ from time to time and from economy to economy.

The model, which is developed in Chapter III, provides for either type of concept or in fact anything in between by introducing a parameter, q, which specifies the proportion of investment income which has to be deducted from the available savings. This is a somewhat artificial device. It is introduced largely to make it easier to work out how a model would behave if one used one savings concept or the other, in the first instance. And, if one chooses to use a hybrid, this is possible too.

The model as presented is not intended to be anything more than illustrative. It is based on the simple Harrod-Domar prototype and is therefore very much an abstraction. Its purpose is purely expository. It does not pretend to mimic reality but only tries to illustrate, as graphically as possible, the way things would work, given some highly simplified assumptions (such as the constancy of the capital-output ratio). This can be a useful device. Many people were taught

3

the Newtonian mechanics about a falling object in a vacuum ($v = gt$ and all that). Although we do not live in a vacuum (at any rate, a physical one), it is a useful intellectual discipline; no one need be under any illusion that that is how a feather falls. The purpose of expository models of this kind has been well described by Professor Mahalanobis: "I find simple models useful in planning (just as the thermo-dynamical approach is useful in physics) in revealing the broad characteristics of the system under consideration without getting lost in the details."[2]

Consequently the model, in its initial form, has no frills. It is a very simple one indeed, since it is not even based on a marginal savings concept; or, rather, it would be more correct to say that the marginal savings rate is assumed to be equal to the initial average rate. This is a minor simplification, not a fundamental one, which makes it easier to illustrate what follows in Chapter IV. In this chapter there is a comparison between the model in its domestic savings version and in its national savings version. Numerical examples are followed by an explanation of the way in which the difference arises. This can most readily be explained in terms of a single inflow of capital, an exercise which has been performed before but, as far as we can see, incorrectly.[3] In either of the versions or in the more general one adopted here external assistance has the same immediate or direct effect on income. But the incremental savings out of this incremental income, compounded over time, are different; thus the difference lies in this indirect effect on income.[4]

Chapter V is by way of being a homily. It is altogether too easy to construct an expository model of this kind and to make far-reaching deductions from it. This chapter uses this particular type of model to make a point which can perhaps be made more generally. Almost any model is bound to rest on certain assumptions, simple or esoteric. This fact, and the dangers that stem from it, have been so

---

[2] "The Approach of Operational Research to Planning in India," *Sankhya*, (December 1955).

[3] See A. Qayum, "Long Term Economic Criteria for Foreign Loans," *The Economical Journal*, LXXVI, No. 302, (June 1966), where the domestic savings version is implicitly used without saying so. This fact was pointed out by Charles Kennedy in a note in the same journal in September 1967. See also Annex 4.

[4] It is because we are concerned with the effect of external aid *per se* that the level of the initial average savings rate is, at this point, irrelevant.

4

often stated that they require no repetition.[5] What does perhaps need stating is that the burden of pointing out the implications of these assumptions rests with the model-builder, as far as he is able to do so. Otherwise, he runs the risk that others, less informed, will invest the model with an oracular significance which it cannot bear. The case presented here, where the use of a certain type of conventional national accounting concept leads to a highly specific assumption, is merely a case in point and rather a simple one.

Finally, the paper ends with Chapter VI which introduces a range of additional complications into the model. Whether these additional complications are worthwhile is somewhat questionable. It is possible that they may prove useful from time to time, but it is all too easy to succumb to the temptation to complicate in the belief that this is a concession to reality. One or two concessions of this kind do not necessarily bring one any closer to reality and may at the same time liberate one from knowing what one is doing. The urge to complicate is often provoked by the temptation to use expository models as predictive tools, in spite of the innumerable assumptions inherent in the model. Besides smacking of pseudo-science, this sort of procedure misses one of the main purposes of the expository model, namely, as a policy instrument, a way of illuminating choices.

---

[5] See for example Raymond Vernon, "Comprehensive Model-Building in the Planning Process: The Case of the Less-Developed Economies," *The Economic Journal*, (March 1966); and Louis Lefeber, "Notes on the Bergsman-Manne Model and the Uses of Planning Models," *The Economic Weekly*, (December 25, 1965).

II

THE ACCUMULATION FUNCTION: A NECESSARY TOOL

The purpose of this section is to introduce a practical working tool. Any model in which one or more variables grows at a constant rate per annum (or any other period) will necessarily involve certain mathematical expressions. The more interaction between variables, the more complicated and tedious to the reader these expressions will be and the easier it will be to lose sight of what is going on. If we can devise a simple notation and simple rules to deal with them, so much the better.

Two of these expressions are familiar to anyone who uses compound interest tables:

Amount at compound interest $\qquad (1 + i)^n$

Amount of an annuity $\qquad \dfrac{(1 + i)^n - 1}{i}$

The first formula expresses what an amount of 1 will grow to in n periods whether it be an investment growing at an interest rate of i per annum or an economy at the same rate of growth.[1]

---

[1] Throughout this paper interest is assumed to be paid annually.

The second formula gives the amount that n successive investments of 1 each per annum will amount to at the time of the last investment if each grows at interest rate i. Specifically:

$$\sum_{t=1}^{n} (1 + i)^{t-1} = \frac{(1 + i)^n - 1}{i} \tag{1}$$

However we might and, in fact, we will wish to consider a series of investments, which are not equal but are themselves growing at a different rate, say, r. Then the question will be what is the accumulated sum of these successive and increasing investments each with its accumulated interest. We may represent the problem thus:

Year	Investment	Compound interest factor in year n	Product
1	1	$(1 + i)^{n-1}$	$(1 + i)^{n-1}$
2	$(1 + r)$	$(1 + i)^{n-2}$	$(1 + r)(1 + i)^{n-2}$
—	—	—	—
n	$(1 + r)^{n-1}$	1	$(1 + r)^{n-1}$

The investment 1 in year 1 has $(n - 1)$ years in which to accumulate interest; hence it is multiplied by $(1 + i)^{n-1}$. The investment in year 2 is $(1 + r)$, but it only has $(n - 2)$ years to grow; hence the compound interest factor is $(1 + i)^{n-2}$. And so on. The sum of the expressions in the last column is:

$$\sum_{t=1}^{n} (1 + r)^{t-1} (1 + i)^{n-t} = \frac{(1 + i)^n - (1 + r)^n}{(i - r)} \tag{2}$$

This is, in fact, a more generalized version of the amount of an annuity, since the latter can be derived simply by putting $r = 0$.

It is clear from the symmetry of the expression on the right-hand side that we can substitute i and r for each other. A series of investments growing at a rate i per annum, which accumulate interest at r per annum, will grow to the same amount. Specifically:

$$\sum_{t=1}^{n} (1 + i)^{t-1} (1 + r)^{n-t} = \frac{(1 + r)^n - (1 + i)^n}{(r - i)} \tag{3}$$

The right-hand side of either (2) or (3) may be written as follows:

$$\frac{(1 + r)^n}{(r - i)} + \frac{(1 + i)^n}{(i - r)} \qquad (4)$$

Expressions like this and even more complicated ones will recur constantly. This is why we need a notation.

Notation and Definition of the Accumulation Function

We shall now define the accumulation function and the notation to be used as follows:

Description	Notation[2]		Formula	
First generation	$\mathbf{I}_n$	$=$	$(1 + i)^n$	(5)
Second generation	$\mathbf{IR}_n$	$=$	$\dfrac{(1 + i)^n}{(i - r)} + \dfrac{(1 + r)^n}{(r - i)}$	(6)

The first of these is simply the compound interest formula. The second is the expression (4) we met just above. It follows from (3) that:

$$\sum_{t=1}^{n} \mathbf{I}_{t-1} (1 + r)^{n-t} = \mathbf{IR}_n \qquad (7)$$

This is the rule for proceeding from the first generation to the second. We shall also apply the same rule in defining a third generation. We proceed from the second to the third as follows:

$$\sum_{t=1}^{n} \mathbf{IR}_{t-1} (1 + j)^{n-t} = \mathbf{IRJ}_n \qquad (8)$$

This third generation function may also be expressed in the same way as the first and second generation ones as follows:

$$\mathbf{IRJ}_n = \frac{(1 + i)^n}{(i - r)(i - j)} + \frac{(1 + r)^n}{(r - i)(r - j)} + \frac{(1 + j)^n}{(j - r)(j - i)} \qquad (9)$$

It was possible to explain, in reasonably everyday terms, the significance of the second generation function as the accumulated

---

[2] Boldface [I] has been adopted for printing purposes. In typescript we use I̲. When a subscript follows a group of letters in boldface, e.g. $\mathbf{IR}_n$, the subscript refers to all the letters in the group, e.g. I and R.

amount of a series of investments growing at a particular rate, together with interest compounded at a different rate. It is not possible to describe the third generation function in the same simple way. We can do no more than express in words what equation (8) says in symbols, namely, that the third generation function is the result of investing an amount equal to the second generation function at yet a third rate of return. It will be observed from the symmetry of equation (9) that the order in which the three rates of return appear makes no difference. $\mathbf{RIJ}_n$ is equal to $\mathbf{IJR}_n$. Subsequently, following sound theatrical practice, the characters will usually be placed in the order of their appearance, but this is not actually necessary.

There is, in fact, a regular pattern which would enable us to write out directly an expression for each generation defined by accumulating the previous one, as in (7) or (8). But we shall only need three generations here.

It should be emphasized that we have merely introduced a notation for the purpose of brevity and, hopefully, clarity.[3] The notation $\mathbf{RIJ}_n$ does not mean, in any sense, that $\mathbf{R}$ is multiplied by $\mathbf{I}$ and $\mathbf{J}$. It only means what it is defined to mean, namely the sum expressed in (9). Rules can be developed for treating these bold letters as a kind of mathematical operator, but it is not necessary to go into them here. These, together with proofs of identities, are described in Annex 1.[4]

Accumulation will occur in subsequent chapters because of the normal process of adding compound interest or because of the process of saving and reinvestment or because of the introduction of an arbitrary growth rate; these rates are usually denoted by i, j, and r respectively. The advantage of the notation is that, each time there is an additional accumulation process, all one has to do is to add the appropriate letter to whatever expressions are being accumulated. With a little familiarity, working with the function in this form can

---

[3] An application to published material is given in Annex 4.

[4] There is a complete parallel with exponential functions and successive integration:

$$\mathbf{R}_t = e^{rt}; \ \mathbf{RI}_t = \frac{e^{rt} - e^{it}}{(r - i)};$$

and so on.

become a fairly simple business. Care must be exercised as to whether the suffix should be $(n - 1)$ or n or $(n + 1)$, but this can usually be checked by putting $n = 0$ or 1.

In order to give the reader an idea of the order of magnitude of these unfamiliar expressions, values of the second generation function are shown in the annexed tables for periods 5, 10, 15, 20, and 25 years and for various rates of interest and growth. Tables for the third generation function are also included for the same periods, but only for those cases where one of the three growth rates is zero.

The rest of this chapter is concerned with a few special applications: the values of the function with suffixes such as 0 and 1, the important case of a zero growth rate, and the formula when two or more rates are equal.

Initial Values

The initial values of the function up to the third generation are as follows (a generalized proof is given in Annex 1d):

$$I_1 = 1 + i \qquad IR_2 = 2 + i + r \qquad IRJ_3 = 3 + i + r + j$$
$$I_0 = 1 \qquad IR_1 = 1 \qquad IRJ_2 = 1$$
$$IR_0 = 0 \qquad IRJ_1 = 0$$
$$IRJ_0 = 0$$

Many of these are self-evident, but the reader might reasonably ask how it is that the accumulation function, which is the sum of a number of positive elements, could ever be zero. The answer is simply that, except for the first generation, the function with suffix zero is the sum of no elements. If we put $n = 0$ in equation (7), we get a meaningless sum. Conventionally we put this sum equal to zero. All the other zero values follow from this.

In fact there is a practical significance where there is a one-year lag between one event and another. Investment in one year (year 0) yields income the next (year 1); out of this income there are reinvested savings which yield income in the following year (year 2). The indirect income so created will, in fact, be represented by a third generation function which equals zero for $n = 0$ and 1.

Zero Growth Rate

We will often need to use a zero growth rate in the function. This we will designate simply by **O**. Accumulation at zero growth rate is merely a cumbersome synonym for summation.

By putting $i = 0$ in (5), (6) and (9), it is easy to show that:

$$\mathbf{O}_n \quad = 1 \tag{10}$$

$$\mathbf{OR}_n \quad = \frac{1}{-r} + \frac{(1+r)^n}{r} \tag{11}$$

$$\mathbf{ORJ}_n = \frac{1}{rj} + \frac{(1+r)^n}{r(r-j)} + \frac{(1+j)^n}{j(j-r)} \tag{12}$$

The second of these is simply the formula (1) for the amount of an annuity, since it equals:

$$\frac{(1+r)^n - 1}{r}$$

This can be interpreted as either (i) a constant amount each year accumulated at an interest rate of r, or (ii) an amount growing at a rate r accumulated or summed without interest. An example of the latter, which will emerge later, would be when an increasing amount is borrowed each year. If the rate of increase is r, the amount of the resulting debt is simply the sum of $\mathbf{R}_t$ from 0 to $(n-1)$, i.e. $\mathbf{RO}_n$.

Equal Growth Rates

In the special case when $r = i$, the formulae in (6) and (9) plainly do not work. Going back to (7), however, it is clear that:

$$\mathbf{RR}_n = \sum_{t=1}^{n} (1+r)^{t-1} (1+r)^{n-t}$$

$$= \sum_{t=1}^{n} (1+r)^{n-1}$$

$$= n (1+r)^{n-1} \tag{13}$$

It is fairly easy to show in a similar way that:

$$\mathbf{RRR}_n = \frac{n (n-1)}{2} (1+r)^{n-2} \tag{14}$$

Two special cases when the growth rate is zero, are:

$$\mathbf{OO}_n \ = n$$
$$\mathbf{OOO}_n = \frac{n\,(n-1)}{2}$$

The first is simply the sum of n times one and the second of $0 + 1 + 2 \ldots + (n-1)$.

III

SAVINGS MODELS: RULES OF THE GAME

The model used is, as we said, based on the simple Harrod-Domar prototype. In this chapter we shall devise rules, which will form a sort of do-it-yourself kit. These will not only serve for the version in which the savings rate is fixed in relation to gross domestic product and one in which it is fixed in relation to gross national product; they will also serve for other assumptions about the savings rate which lie between.

In the simplest type of model without external aid, an economy will grow at a rate (j) determined by the savings rate (s) and the capital-output ratio (k); $s = kj$. This rate of growth, j, is an important element in the model. When there is external aid it will not be the actual rate of growth. It has been called, as sparingly as possible, the "intrinsic rate of growth." It can have an initial and a marginal version.

Two preliminary remarks must be made about this exercise. First, debt is used as a term of art. It includes conventional and nonconventional loans, grants and equity investment. Grants do not present a problem since they are debts at zero interest; "outstanding debt" then includes accumulated grants. Equity investment, however, is

13

another matter. Unless we believe that the return on equity investment is reasonably constant over time, the model needs modification.

Secondly, everything in the model is in gross terms, i.e. not net
of depreciation. Strictly speaking, one should then make an allowance
for replacement of capital. This presents no problem when investment grows at a constant rate because replacement can easily be
incorporated in the capital-output ratio. This is not true at variable
growth rates. This is a lacuna, for which one can think of various
weak excuses, but it is perhaps better to just plead guilty and pass
on.[1]

Some Definitions and Relationships

We shall define the inflow of external capital *before* deduction of
investment income payments abroad as the flow of *financial* resources
and the inflow of external capital *after* deduction of investment
income payments abroad as the flow of *real* resources. We denote
these as F and T respectively.[2] If D is outstanding debt at the
beginning of the year and i the interest rate, then:

$$F = T + iD$$

If V = GDP and Z = GNP, then

$$V = Z + iD$$

If S' = domestic savings and S = national savings,

$$S' = S + iD$$

If I = investment,

$$I = S' + T = S + F$$

Savings Available for Investment

If domestic savings are assumed to be a constant proportion s'
of GDP (or, alternatively, the marginal rate equals the average):

$$S' = s'V$$

---

[1] An indication of the nature of the adjustment is given in Annex 4.

[2] The inflow of external capital is defined *net* of amortization payments here and
throughout the rest of the paper.

If, on the other hand, national savings are assumed to be a constant proportion s of GNP:

$$S = sZ$$

Investment in the two cases will be equal to:

(a) $$s'V + F - iD$$

(b) $$sZ + F = sV + F - siD$$

The difference, in form, is that in the one case the whole of interest has to be deducted from the available internal savings and external inflow of capital and, in the other, only a part.

We may generalize this by adopting yet a third form:

(c) $$sV + F - qiD$$

In this form q expresses more generally the proportion of interest which has to be deducted. In the two cases (a) and (b) above, $q = 1$ and $q = s$. We could also imagine a case where, for example, interest payments were wholly at the expense of consumption, in which case $q = 0$. For the present, the question whether this "q" has any economic significance will be ducked. The justification is the wholly pragmatic one that it makes the model-building easier.

Assumptions for the Model

We could approach the construction of a model in either of two ways. We could assume a certain pattern of behavior of GDP or GNP, e.g. a constant growth rate, and see what pattern of external aid is required to achieve this. Alternatively, we could assume a certain pattern of external flow of resources and see what happens to GDP and GNP as a consequence.

Purely for the purposes of building the model, we shall do the latter; once the rules have been established, the assumptions can readily be varied.

Specifically, we assume that the flow of financial resources (F) grows at a constant rate r per annum:

$$F_n = F_0 \mathbf{R}_n$$

However, since we shall have occasion to divide F_0 by the capital-output ratio k, we shall introduce a constant a, such that $F_0 = ka$. Hence:

$$F_n = ka\mathbf{R}_n$$

We shall further assume that investment is in the form denoted above by (c).

The Growth of Debt

If debt outstanding initially is nil, the amount of outstanding debt at the beginning of any year is simply the sum of the annual flows of financial resources $(ka\mathbf{R}_t)$. The sum is expressed by adding $\mathbf{O}$ (see Chapter II):

$$D_n = ka\mathbf{RO}_n$$
$$\text{Interest} = kai\mathbf{RO}_n$$

The Internal Contribution to Growth of GDP

If there were no external aid and therefore no debt and no interest, the economy would grow at the intrinsic rate of growth $s/k = j$. Hence we would have:

$$V_n = V_0\mathbf{J}_n$$

The External Contribution to Growth of GDP (at nil interest)

The increment in income as a result of each inflow of external aid $ka\mathbf{R}_t$ in year t is equal to $a\mathbf{R}_t$ the following year $(t + 1)$. But each increment in income will itself grow at a rate j for the remaining $n - (t + 1)$ years. The aggregate of all the increments in year n is, as we might now expect, the result of accumulating $a\mathbf{R}_t$ at a rate j, i.e.:[3]

$$a\mathbf{RJ}_n$$

---

[3] The sum of the contributions of all investments from year $t = 0$ to year $t = n - 1$ will be:

$$\sum_{t=0}^{n-1} a\mathbf{R}_t (1 + j)^{n-t-1}$$

$$= \sum_{t=1}^{n} a\mathbf{R}_{t-1} (1 + j)^{n-t}$$

$$= a\mathbf{RJ}_n$$

The Deduction from Savings for Interest

Part of interest each year has to be deducted from available savings. In year t the deduction is equal to q times interest in that year:

$$qkai\mathbf{RO}_t$$

In effect this is a negative inflow of capital. Consequently, the accumulated deduction from GDP in year n follows the same rule as above. We divide by k and accumulate at a rate j. Hence the deduction equals:

$$- qai\mathbf{ROJ}_n$$

Recapitulation

Bringing all these parts together, we have the following expression for GDP:

$$V_n = V_0\mathbf{J}_n + a\mathbf{RJ}_n - qai\mathbf{ROJ}_n$$

The rules are, therefore, as follows:

(i) The original GDP is accumulated at a rate j to get the internal contribution to GDP.

(ii) The flow of financial resources *less* that part of interest assumed to be a deduction from savings is accumulated at a rate j and divided by k. This gives the external contribution to GDP.

(iii) To obtain GNP or the external contribution to it, we simply deduct interest ($kai\mathbf{RO}$).

In Table 1 (over the page), we set forth the expression for GDP and GNP for the generalized version and for $q = 1$ (domestic savings basis) and $q = s$ (national savings basis).[4]

---

[4] When $q = s$ a simplification of GNP is possible, using the fact, proved in Annex 1c, that $j\mathbf{ROJ} = (\mathbf{RJ} - \mathbf{RO})$.

The external contribution $= a\mathbf{RJ} - ais\mathbf{ROJ} - kai\mathbf{RO}$
$\qquad\qquad\qquad\qquad = a\mathbf{RJ} - kjai\mathbf{ROJ} - kai\mathbf{RO}$
$\qquad\qquad\qquad\qquad = a\mathbf{RJ} - kai(\mathbf{RJ} - \mathbf{RO}) - kai\mathbf{RO}$
$\qquad\qquad\qquad\qquad = a\mathbf{RJ}\,(1 - ki)$

17

TABLE 1: Generalized Model (Constant Savings Rate)

Description	Formula
Debt outstanding at beginning of year[a] (D_n)	$ka\mathbf{RO}$
Debt interest[a] (iD_n)	$kai\mathbf{RO}$
Flow of financial resources (F_n)	$ka\mathbf{R}$
GDP (V_n)	
(i) General	$V_0\mathbf{J} + a\mathbf{RJ} - qai\mathbf{ROJ}$
(ii) $q = 1$	$V_0\mathbf{J} + a\mathbf{RJ} - ai\mathbf{ROJ}$
(iii) $q = s$	$V_0\mathbf{J} + a\mathbf{RJ} - ais\mathbf{ROJ}$
GNP (Z_n)	
(i) General	$V_0\mathbf{J} + a\mathbf{RJ} - qai\mathbf{ROJ} - kai\mathbf{RO}$
(ii) $q = 1$	$V_0\mathbf{J} + a\mathbf{RJ} - ai\mathbf{ROJ} - kai\mathbf{RO}$
(iii) $q = s$	$V_0\mathbf{J} + a\mathbf{RJ}\,(1 - ki)$

[a] Assuming no initial debt $(D_0 = 0)$.

The implications of one or another assumption will be examined in the next chapter. In this table and henceforth, we drop the suffix n, it being understood that $\mathbf{RO}$, for example, stands for $\mathbf{RO}_n$.

IV

THE MODEL ON DIFFERENT ASSUMPTIONS
ABOUT SAVINGS

It is obvious from the previous chapter that the model behaves differently according to the assumptions one makes about the proportion (q) of investment income which has to be deducted from available savings. In this section we shall compare its behavior for $q = 1$ and $q = s$, i.e. on the basis of a constant domestic and national savings ratio respectively, and we shall try to explain what lies behind the difference.

Four numerical examples have been worked out, which are shown in tables below and, graphically, in a chart. They are all based on the simplest version of the model, that is, without initial conditions. In order to illustrate what happens under different circumstances, the parameters are changed from one example to another. But, in each example, the behavior of the two models is compared under conditions which are identical except for the value of q.

In each example, the initial flow of financial resources, the rate at which it grows and the interest rate are all the same. The same capital-output ratio is used for both versions and the same initial volume of savings. This means that initially the domestic savings ratio and the national savings ratio are the same, there being no

19

interest on debt. From then on, if one of them is fixed, they part company.

In Example 1, the intrinsic rate of growth of the economy (j) is higher than either the rate of growth of external aid (r) or the interest rate (i). Ultimately external aid becomes negligible and so does interest on debt. If the national savings ratio is fixed, the domestic savings ratio becomes a little larger. If the domestic savings ratio is fixed, the national savings ratio becomes a little smaller. The only thing perhaps worth noting is that, for a given fixed national savings ratio, the external contribution to GNP is substantially higher than for the same fixed domestic savings ratio. That there would be a difference is, of course, to be expected.

In Example 2, the intrinsic rate of growth of the economy (j) is now less than the rate of growth of aid (r), but still higher than the interest rate (i). In this event, aid gradually increases as a proportion of GNP but there is a limit. Furthermore, as a consequence, debt interest does the same. Thus the gap between the two savings ratios widens continuously. On the domestic savings basis, the gap widens considerably more, because aid as a percentage of GNP grows faster and so therefore does interest on debt.

The external contribution to GNP is not very different for either model from what it was in the previous example. This follows from two facts about the parameters chosen. First the initial amount of aid, when divided by the capital output ratio, i.e. a, is the same. Secondly, the value of the external contribution depends heavily, though not wholly, on **RJ**. But in fact r and j have simply been interchanged so that the value remains the same.

EXAMPLE 1: Intrinsic Rate of Growth higher than Growth of Aid or Interest Rate

	Year 0	Year 10	Year 25	Year 50	Limit
Common features					
Aid[a]	3.0	4.4	8.0	21.3	...
Debt interest	—	1.1	3.7	13.7	...
National savings basis					
GNP: total	100.0	176.4	404.2	1,543.6	...
external contribution	—	13.5	65.6	396.9	...
Savings ratio: national, %	15.0	15.0	15.0	15.0	15.0
domestic, %	15.0	15.0	15.8	15.7	15.0
Aid as percent of GNP	3.0	2.5	2.0	1.4	0
Debt interest as percent of GNP	—	0.6	0.9	0.9	0
Domestic savings basis					
GNP: total	100.0	175.0	388.7	1,399.1	...
external contribution	—	12.1	50.1	252.4	...
Savings ratio: national, %	15.0	14.5	14.2	14.2	15.0
domestic, %	15.0	15.0	15.0	15.0	15.0
Aid as percent of GNP	3.0	2.5	2.1	1.5	0
Debt interest as percent of GNP	—	0.6	1.0	1.0	0

[a] Flow of financial resources.

$$Values: k = 3 \qquad j = .05$$
$$a = 1 \qquad i = .03$$
$$s = .15 \qquad r = .04$$

EXAMPLE 2: Intrinsic Rate of Growth less than Rate of Growth of Aid but more than Interest Rate

	Year 0	Year 10	Year 25	Year 50	Limit
Common features					
Aid[a]	4.0	6.5	13.5	45.9	...
Debt interest	—	1.5	5.7	25.1	...
National savings basis					
GNP: total	100.0	161.1	330.0	1,094.4	...
external contribution	—	13.1	63.4	383.7	...
Savings ratio: national, %	16.0	16.0	16.0	16.0	16.0
domestic, %	16.0	16.8	17.4	17.9	18.2
Aid as percent of GNP	4.0	4.0	4.1	4.2	4.5
Debt interest as percent of GNP	—	0.9	1.7	2.3	2.7
Domestic savings basis					
GNP: total	100.0	159.7	314.7	951.6	...
external contribution	—	11.6	48.1	240.9	...
Savings ratio: national, %	16.0	15.2	14.5	13.8	10.6
domestic, %	16.0	16.0	16.0	16.0	16.0
Aid as percent of GNP	4.0	4.1	4.3	4.8	10.6
Debt interest as percent of GNP	—	0.9	1.8	2.6	6.4

[a] Flow of financial resources.

$$Values: k = 4 \qquad j = .04$$
$$a = 1 \qquad i = .03$$
$$s = .16 \qquad r = .05$$

Example 3 is no different from the second, except for the interest rate, which has been raised from 3 to 5 percent and is now equal to the rate of growth of aid (r). This means that the flow of real resources remains constant. On a national savings basis, this makes a perceptible difference to the external contribution to GNP, but most of it is explainable on the grounds that there is more interest to subtract. The various ratios in the table are somewhat higher, but not much.

However, on a domestic savings basis, the effect is drastic. In fifty years the external contribution to GNP is barely more than half what it was in the previous example. If one were to carry this model to its ultimate, but absurd, conclusion, debt interest would eventually become larger than GDP and GNP would become negative.

The fourth example is a somewhat different variant of the third. In this, there is no increase in aid from year to year ($r = 0$). The interest rate (i) is again 5 percent and the intrinsic rate of growth (j) 3 percent. On a national savings basis, nothing very dramatic happens. The external contribution to GNP, being based on a static volume of aid, is of course quite small in comparison to previous examples and eventually would become negligible.

On a domestic savings basis, somewhat the same thing happens as on a national savings basis, in that external aid ultimately becomes unimportant. But not only is the external contribution to GNP very small. By the end of fifty years it is actually negative and in fact will continue to be thereafter. It remains to be seen just how these rather strange results of the model occur.

EXAMPLE 3: Intrinsic Rate of Growth less than Rate of Growth of Aid or Interest Rate, which are Equal

	Year 0	Year 10	Year 25	Year 50	Limit
Common features					
Aid[a]	4.0	6.5	13.5	45.9	...
Debt interest	—	2.5	9.5	41.9	...
National savings basis					
GNP: total	100.0	159.9	324.2	1,059.6	...
external contribution	—	11.9	57.6	348.9	...
Savings ratio: national, %	16.0	16.0	16.0	16.0	16.0
domestic, %	16.0	17.3	18.4	19.2	20.0
Aid as percent of GNP	4.0	4.1	4.2	4.3	5.0
Debt interest as percent of GNP	—	1.6	2.9	4.0	5.0
Domestic savings basis					
GNP: total	100.0	157.5	298.7	821.5	...
external contribution	—	9.5	32.1	110.8	...
Savings ratio: national, %	16.0	14.7	13.3	11.7	[b]
domestic, %	16.0	16.0	16.0	16.0	[b]
Aid as percent of GNP	4.0	4.1	4.5	5.6	[b]
Debt interest as percent of GNP	—	1.6	3.2	5.1	[b]

[a] Flow of financial resources.
[b] GNP becomes negative.

Values: $k = 4$ $j = .04$
         $a = 1$ $i = .05$
         $s = .16$ $r = .05$

EXAMPLE 4: Intrinsic Rate of Growth is less than Interest Rate, with Aid Static

	Year 0	Year 10	Year 25	Year 50	Limit
Common features					
Aid[a]	4.0	4.0	4.0	4.0	...
Debt interest	—	2.0	5.0	10.0	...
National savings basis					
GNP: total	100.0	143.6	238.5	528.6	...
external contribution	—	9.2	29.2	90.2	...
Savings ratio: national, %	12.0	12.0	12.0	12.0	12.0
domestic, %	12.0	13.2	13.8	13.6	12.0
Aid as percent of GNP	4.0	2.8	1.7	0.8	0
Debt interest percent of GNP	—	1.4	2.1	1.9	0
Domestic savings basis					
GNP: total	100.0	141.4	221.7	436.5	...
external contribution	—	7.0	12.4	−1.9	...
Savings ratio: national, %	12.0	10.8	10.0	10.0	12.0
domestic, %	12.0	12.0	12.0	12.0	12.0
Aid as percent of GNP	4.0	2.8	1.8	0.9	0
Debt interest as percent of GNP	—	1.4	2.3	2.3	0

[a] Flow of financial resources.

Values: $k = 4$ $j = .03$
         $a = 1$ $i = .05$
         $s = .12$ $r = 0$

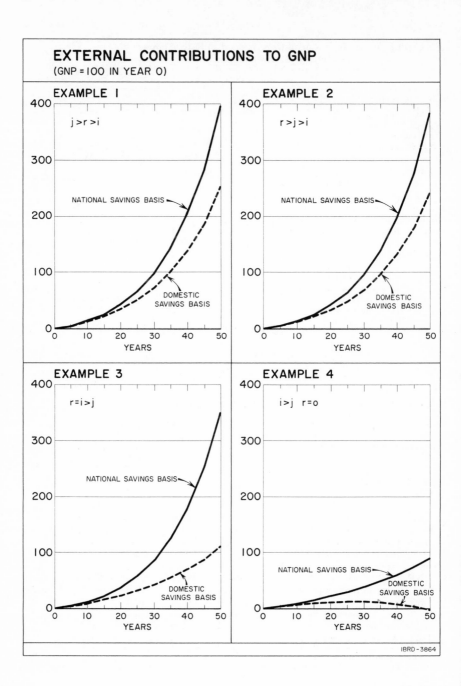

EXTERNAL CONTRIBUTIONS TO GNP
(GNP = 100 IN YEAR 0)

EXAMPLE 1
j > r > i
NATIONAL SAVINGS BASIS
DOMESTIC SAVINGS BASIS
YEARS

EXAMPLE 2
r > j > i
NATIONAL SAVINGS BASIS
DOMESTIC SAVINGS BASIS
YEARS

EXAMPLE 3
r = i > j
NATIONAL SAVINGS BASIS
DOMESTIC SAVINGS BASIS
YEARS

EXAMPLE 4
i > j r = o
NATIONAL SAVINGS BASIS
DOMESTIC SAVINGS BASIS
YEARS

IBRD - 3864

24

How the Difference Arises

To understand what happens, we shall examine the consequences of a single external investment of an amount ka made in year 0. The consequences the following year are shown under the first heading, A, in Table 2. The contribution to GDP is, of course, a. The contribution to savings available for investment depends on q. If qi exceeds j, it will be negative.

TABLE 2: The Effect of a Single Investment

External aid (year 0)	ka
Annual interest payments thereafter	kai
A. Consequences in year 1	
Addition to GDP	a
Addition to domestic savings	as
Deduction for interest	$qkai$
Addition to available savings	$a(s - kqi) = ka(j - qi)$
B. Consequences in year $(n + 1)$	
Addition to GDP	$a\mathbf{J} - qai\mathbf{OJ}$
of which:	
Direct addition	a
Indirect addition	$a(j - qi)\mathbf{OJ}$

On a domestic savings basis ($q = 1$), the amount available for investment will be negative, if the rate of interest (i) exceeds the intrinsic rate of growth (j).[1] This is perfectly possible. On a national savings basis ($q = s$), however, the available savings will equal $as(1 - ki)$.[2] Unless the capital-output ratio and the interest rate are both very high (e.g. 10 and 0.10), the contribution will be positive.

Under heading B the effect of the same single investment on GDP after $n + 1$ years is shown. There is a direct addition (the original amount in the first year) and an indirect addition (the result of investments from the savings accumulated over the years). The latter is simply the addition to available savings divided by k and accumulated at a rate j. Whether the indirect addition is positive or negative, it grows in absolute amount.

---

[1] Qayum, *op. cit.*, reaches a different conclusion. For observations on this, see Annex 4.

[2] $ka(j - si) = as - kasi = as(1 - ki)$.

25

In the numerical example given in Table 3, the values of the parameters are the same as in Example 3. Here, i exceeds j. Consequently, investment income payments are larger than domestic savings in the second column (domestic savings basis) and the amount available for investment is negative. In this event, the initial contribution of aid to income is positive, but as time passes, the cumulative effect of the negative addition to available savings gets larger and larger. On a national savings basis, there is the same cumulative effect but it is positive.

The difference in the contribution of the single investment to GDP after twenty-five years is shown under heading B. The addition to savings (in the first column) of 0.128 in a single year by itself gives rise—at a capital-output ratio of 4—to additional income of 0.032. This is not large, but it happens every year and is cumulative at the growth rate j, here 4 percent. The amount of an annuity at this rate after twenty-four years is 39.1. Hence the indirect effect is by that time 1.25, much greater than the direct. Similarly the very small negative effect on savings in the second column assumes considerable importance after twenty-five years. In thirty-eight years the negative indirect effect would exceed the positive direct one.

On a domestic savings basis, therefore, the model tacitly assumes that, where i exceeds j, the contribution to GDP of each external

TABLE 3: The Effect of a Single Investment: Numerical Example

	National savings basis	Domestic savings basis
External aid (year 0)	4.00	4.00
Annual interest payments thereafter	0.20	0.20
A. Consequences in year 1		
Addition to GDP	1.00	1.00
Addition to domestic savings	0.160	0.16
Deduction for interest	0.032	0.20
Addition to available savings	0.128	−0.04
B. Consequences in year 25		
Addition to GDP	2.25	0.61
of which:		
Direct addition	1.00	1.00
Indirect addition	1.25	−0.39

Values: $a = 1$	$j = 0.04$	
$k = 4$	$i = 0.05$	
$s = 0.16$	$r = 0.05$	

investment is ultimately negative. This conclusion is true even if the marginal rate of savings does not equal the initial average. The external contribution is only affected by the marginal rate.

Initial Savings Rate

If we assume an initial savings rate (s_0), savings and therefore investment are less than in the previous model in the initial year and in each subsequent year by a constant amount $V_0(s - s_0)$. If there were to be an external investment of this amount each year at no interest cost, the growth of GDP would be the same as before (i.e. at a rate of j). The effect is thus similar to that of external investment except that it is negative.

The consequences are the same as if there were a negative transfer of financial resources (without interest) equivalent to:

$$F = V_0(s - s_0)$$
$$= V_0(s - s_0)\ \mathbf{O} \qquad (\text{since } \mathbf{O} = 1)$$

If we define an initial intrinsic rate of growth by $s_0 = kj_0$, the adjustment to GDP is found by applying the rule of dividing by k and accumulating at a rate j. Hence the adjustment will be:

$$- V_0(j - j_0)\mathbf{OJ}$$

In total, internal contribution to GDP is:

$$V = V_0\mathbf{J} - V_0(j - j_0)\mathbf{OJ}$$
$$= V_0 + V_0 j_0 \mathbf{OJ}$$

Without aid, the economy grows initially at a rate j_0, but growth gradually creeps up to the marginal rate j. But the external contribution will be unaffected.

27

The Fate of the External Contribution

The contribution of a single investment to GDP (or GNP) will, as we have seen, ultimately become negative if qi exceeds j. This does not necessarily mean that the contributions of all investments will at any one time be negative. At any one time, there will be some positive contributions from the most recent external investments and some negative ones from earlier ones. Whether the overall external contribution to GNP becomes negative and whether this negative amount eventually is large enough to swamp the internal contribution depends on a variety of circumstances. These are described in this section, which may readily be skipped by the reader not interested in such curiosities.

We can best examine what happens by looking at the expression for GNP in Table 1 (page 18), modified for the existence of an initial savings rate as described in the previous section. Two cases may be distinguished in the long run. Either j exceeds r, in which case the coefficient of **J** will be the governing factor; or the reverse, in which case it will be the coefficient of **R**. If for convenience we write h for qi, these coefficients are:

Coefficient of	Internal contribution	External contribution
J	$\dfrac{V_0 j_0}{j}$	$\dfrac{a}{(j-r)} \cdot \dfrac{(j-h)}{j}$
R	—	$\dfrac{a}{(r-j)} \cdot \dfrac{(r-h)}{r} - \dfrac{kai}{r}$

Thus, in the first case, if $h > j > r$, the external contribution will be negative, but it will only be large enough to swamp the internal, if:

$$V_0 j_0 (j-r) < a(h-j)$$

In the second case, where both r and h exceed j, the external contribution will be negative if:

$$(r-j)ki > (r-h)$$
$$\text{or } (h-j) > (r-j)(1-ki)$$

We may now sum this up. When h exceeds j, in the long run the fate of the external contribution and of GNP will be as follows:

Relation between r and j	External contribution	GNP
$-\dfrac{a}{V_0 j_0} > \dfrac{(r-j)}{(h-j)}$	Negative	Positive
$\dfrac{1}{1-ki} > \dfrac{(r-j)}{(h-j)} > -\dfrac{a}{V_0 j_0}$	Negative	Negative
$\dfrac{(r-j)}{(h-j)} > \dfrac{1}{1-ki}$	Positive	Positive

In other words, if aid grows slowly, i.e. if r is less than j, the external contribution will ultimately become negative. But it will not necessarily be sufficiently large to swamp the internal contribution. For that to happen, given the initial value of the flow of financial resources, its rate of growth must be of a certain size. This makes sense. If aid is only growing slowly, the new positive contributions are not big enough to offset the accumulation of old negative ones. This is hardly satisfactory, but it is not disastrous, because the intrinsic growth of the economy is sufficient to offset the negative effects of aid.

Beyond this point, however, we have the intermediate cases. In these cases, which we might roughly term medium growth of aid, the external contribution is not only bound to become negative eventually; it is also bound to swamp the internal contribution.

The last case is fast growth of aid, where r is somewhat in excess of j. There, although the effect of each investment is negative ultimately, the total external contribution is positive. This also makes sense. If aid is growing fast enough, the recent positive contributions outweigh the old negative ones. But it is rather like filling a bathtub with the stopper out.

V

USE AND ABUSE OF THE MODEL

In this section we shall have something to say about the kind of deductions that can and cannot properly be made from a model of this kind. We shall start by making good the promise that the model can, so to speak, be put into reverse. One can start with a target rate of growth of GDP and determine the necessary growth of aid.

If the target rate of growth is r,

$$V = V_0 \mathbf{R}$$

The required expression for F is complicated because not only does the new rate of growth r come into it, but also, qi (which we shall denote as h) because of the effect of interest on savings. If there is an initial savings rate (s_0), the required external investment is:

$$F = V_0(s - s_0)\mathbf{H} + V_0 k(r - j)\, \frac{(r\mathbf{R} - h\mathbf{H})}{r - h}$$

The two parts of this expression[1] fulfil two separate functions. The first part offsets the shortfall in savings because of the lower

---

[1] The reader who does not want to take things for granted will find the proof in Annex 2.

initial savings rate and raises the growth rate to j. The second part raises or lowers it from j to r.

Debt is derived by summing the flow of financial resources (accumulation at zero growth rate):

$$D = V_0(s - s_0)\mathbf{OH} + V_0 k(r - j)\mathbf{RH}$$

"Critical" Interest

Under certain conditions debt will increase faster than GDP. These can readily be identified, namely, that h is greater than r and that the coefficient of $\mathbf{H}$ in the formula for debt is greater than zero, i.e.

$$\frac{j - j_0}{h} > \frac{j - r}{h - r}$$

Or $h = qi > \dfrac{r(j - j_0)}{r - j_0}$

These are also the necessary and sufficient conditions for the flow of financial resources to increase at a rate faster than GDP. In this event, of course, GNP will become negative. This corresponds substantially to the slow growth example in the previous chapter, in which $qi > j > r$. To put it another way, debt becomes insupportable, given qi and j, when r exceeds a certain value. Below that, it is supportable.[2]

The model in the particular case of a domestic savings basis ($q = 1$) has been used by Avramovic and his associates to describe what happens when a target rate of growth is postulated for GDP.[3] In this model, there is again no initial debt, but an initial savings rate. Since $q = 1$, $h = i$. The study identifies a critical interest rate, in those cases where r is less than j, in the form given above, i.e.:

$$i = \frac{r(j - j_0)}{r - j_0}$$

---

[2] There is also a corresponding case to the fast growth of aid case, i.e. the bathtub case. In fact, if r exceeds qi, interest does not outstrip GDP as long as:

$$(r - qi) > ki(r - j)$$

[3] See Dragoslav Avramovic *et al.*, *op. cit.*, especially pp. 166 *et seq.* The argument about a critical interest rate is repeated in I. M. D. Little and J. M. Clifford, *International Aid* (London, 1965), Ch. IX.

But this identification depends entirely on the foundation of a very specific assumption about the value of q, in other words, the behavior of savings. What, in fact, this more restrictive version of the model shows is that, if one assumes that any single increment of aid at an interest rate (i) above the intrinsic rate of growth (j) is ultimately self-defeating, then the cumulative effect is disastrous, if i exceeds a certain critical rate. But is it legitimate to put this tacit assumption into the model?

An Expression of Agnosticism

In plain everyday terms, what the model on a domestic savings basis is saying is this. If a borrower invests what he borrows and then consumes the resulting increment in income beyond the point where there is enough to pay for the interest, he is going to be in trouble. The size of his other income, the pace and the interest rate at which he borrows and the extent of his prodigality all determine the nature of the trouble, which may range from foolishness to disaster.

Whether people, governments or economies actually behave like that is open to serious question. Certainly, in the common case of a large enclave industry, whether it be oil or copper or bananas, it is only our curious habits of national accounting which prevent us from realizing that a sizable part of GDP or of export proceeds never sets foot on shore and is simply not available for consumption. What the country receives is not something *less* something (e.g. exports less investment income), but the difference (taxes and local expenditure). To build a model on the supposition that it is the former is to flout the facts.

This is not to say that there may not be other cases, where economies do exhibit the prodigal behavior described above. But evidence of such behavior is not evidence that it need or will continue indefinitely. There is no reason, *ab initio*, to abandon traditional accounting procedures, in which the cost of capital is treated as a cost by the recipient, either for behavioral or normative reasons. The justification for using a domestic savings basis has been put in these terms:[4]

---

[4] Avramovic *et al. op. cit.*, footnote p. 168.

"This form of presentation is required in order to explore the difference made by differences of interest rate, all the other variables remaining unchanged. If the marginal savings rate linked national (rather than domestic) savings to the increase of GDP, then a constant marginal national savings rate would in fact imply different savings efforts with different assumptions as to the rate of interest."

But this is a semantic trap. What is a saving effort? Whatever it is, why should one not expect it to vary with the rate of interest and, indeed, other circumstances as well?

Where external assistance on a very large scale takes place, the effect may be to reduce either national or domestic savings, in the conventional sense, to near zero or below it.[5] Perhaps, under some circumstances, one should expect investment to be related in some way to total available resources rather than to be, as we formally reckon it, the sum of a "savings effort" and the inflow of capital from abroad. A model on these lines, according to which every increment of external aid would immediately mean lower absolute savings, would be easy to construct. Another critical interest rate could be identified above which the external contribution of aid would become negative. Such a model would show interesting characteristics, but it would have no more validity than its own internal consistency.

We return again to the beginning. An expository model may have considerable value in illuminating how an economy will behave on certain assumptions. But it is necessary to state these assumptions and even that is not enough. Very often, the implications of the assumptions need stating as well. If one looks into alternatives, it may appear that the model has severe limitations. The onus for doing this cannot be placed on the reader; there is no doctrine of *caveat lector*. Before we can have confidence in using such models, even for illustrative purposes and over a comparatively short time, we need to know much more about the inputs.

The next section is devoted to further complications of the model, but whether these complications are worthwhile is another matter. In practice the choice of savings functions, of capital-output and savings ratios at the margin and hence of the marginal intrinsic rate of growth is likely to be rather wide. It is entirely possible that the

---

[5] For example in Jordan, South Korea, and, less recently, Israel.

range of results over a time-horizon such as twenty years will be extremely wide, making hazardous any conclusions about the amount of aid required to reach a specific income goal and the terms on which it is given. Over a somewhat shorter period—say ten years—these marginal rates tend to be of less importance than the initial intrinsic rate of growth (j_0). If there are ways and means of improving the flow of savings into more efficient capital investment and of increasing the efficiency of existing assets, these deserve as much attention. A model may help in this case to put the various alternatives in perspective.

The point is illustrated in Table 4 where, on a national savings basis, various ways of increasing the GNP target by an additional $2\frac{1}{2}$ percent over and above the originally assumed increase of about 53 percent are shown.[6] Since the contribution of aid is small rather drastic changes in the amount or the terms of aid are needed; on the other hand, fairly small changes in current efficiency or "performance" can have the same effect. This is all rather obvious, but needs to be emphasized, if the terms of aid are not invariably to be cast as the residual villain of the piece.

TABLE 4: GNP Growth in 10 Years

GNP	V_0	$V_0 i_0$OJ	aRJ	$-$ kaiRO	$-$ qaiROJ	Total
Base	1,000.0	395.4	162.0	−18.9	−5.4	1,533.1
Changes						
(i) Increase j from 6 to 7%	—	19.1	7.2	—	−0.2	26.1
(ii) Increase j_0 from 3 to 3.2%	—	26.4	—	—	—	26.4
(iii) Increase efficiency of existing assets by 2.5%	25.0	—	—	—	—	25.0
(iv) Increase aid by 20%	—	—	32.4	−3.8	−1.1	27.5
(v) Reduce interest rate to zero	—	—	—	18.9	5.4	24.3
(vi) Change q from s to 1	—	—	—	—	−24.7	−24.7

Values: V_0 = 1000

r = .05	a = 10
j = .06	k = 3
j_0 = .03	s = .18
i = .05	q = .18

---

[6] The difference between the contribution of aid on a national and a domestic basis (line vi, Table 4) is about 25 (out of 1000) in this example, i.e. of the same order of magnitude as the other variations shown.

VI

FURTHER COMPLICATIONS

Having established the rules for the simple version of the models, it is mainly a mechanical matter to introduce additional complications. There are four main possibilities:

(i) Initial debt and interest on debt;

(ii) Initial savings rate, different from the marginal one, but applicable to a growing part of gross product;

(iii) A more complicated function for the growth of aid;

(iv) Differential capital-output ratios and interest rates.

The results of introducing the first two of these are shown in Table 5. The first type of complication is hardly a complication at all. The only requirement is to add initial debt (D_0) and interest $(i_0 D_0)$ to the values previously given in Table 1 and to make a suitable deduction for the effect of initial interest on savings.

We have already explained in Chapter IV that if there is an initial savings rate s_0 applicable to the initial value V_0 of GDP, the necessary adjustment to GDP will be:

$$- V_0(j - j_0)\mathbf{OJ}$$

However, there is no particular reason for us to stop at this point. The savings rate s_0 might be conceived of as applying to a growing

TABLE 5: GDP and GNP with Initial Conditions

Debt	$D_0 + ka\,\mathbf{RO}$
Interest	$i_0D_0 + kai\,\mathbf{RO}$
Flow of financial resources	$ka\,\mathbf{R}$
GDP (V)	$V_0\mathbf{J} - V_0(j - j_0)\mathbf{PJ} + a\,\mathbf{RJ} - qai\,\mathbf{ROJ} - \dfrac{i_0D_0\mathbf{OJ}}{k}$
GNP (Z)	$V - i_0D_0 - kai\,\mathbf{RO}$

amount of GDP, not a static one. For example, it might increase at the same rate as population, say p. In this case, the annual reduction in savings would not be a constant $V_0(s - s_0)\mathbf{O}$ but would be $V_0(s - s_0)\mathbf{P}$. The adjustment in GDP would be:

$$- V_0(j - j_0)\mathbf{PJ}$$

The third complication would amount to supposing that the flow of financial resources is in the following form:

$$F = k(a_1\mathbf{R}_1 + a_2\mathbf{R}_2 + \ldots \text{etc.} \ldots)$$

All we have to do in such a case is to add the comparable terms. Such modifications might be made, where public and private investment are expected to grow at different rates. External public and private investment might also be expected both to have different capital-output ratios from that applied to the intrinsic growth of the economy and to carry different interest rates (or the equivalent) and possibly different effects on savings. If these capital-output ratios were k_1, k_2, and the interest rates i_1, i_2, then:

$$F = k_1a_1\mathbf{R}_1 + k_2a_2\mathbf{R}_2$$

The corresponding external contribution to GNP would be:

$$a_1\mathbf{R}_1\mathbf{J} + a_2\mathbf{R}_2\mathbf{J} - q_1a_1i_1\mathbf{R}_1\mathbf{OJ} - q_2a_2i_2\mathbf{R}_2\mathbf{OJ}$$

A further complication would be to suppose that the lag between investment and income is more than one year. A partial analysis of the case where the lag is two years will be found in Annex 3. It is partial, because it assumes a zero interest rate. To introduce interest would be to complicate matters further without much additional benefit. There are simpler rough devices which can be used, such as taking as one's unit of time not one year, but two or possibly more. In any long-term analysis, a single year has no particular merit as a unit.

36

ANNEX 1

PROPERTIES OF THE
ACCUMULATION FUNCTION

a. Definition

	when $n > 0$	*when* $n = 0$
$(\mathbf{R}_1)_n$	$= (1 + r_1)^n$	$= 1$
$(\mathbf{R}_1\mathbf{R}_2)_n$	$= \sum_1^n (\mathbf{R}_1)_{t-1} (1 + r_2)^{n-t}$	$= 0$
$(\mathbf{R}_1\mathbf{R}_2 \ldots \mathbf{R}_m)_n$	$= \sum_1^n (\mathbf{R}_1\mathbf{R}_2 \ldots \mathbf{R}_{m-1})_{t-1} (1 + r_m)^{n-t} = 0$	

b. Formula

We shall show that:

$(\mathbf{R}_1\mathbf{R}_2 \ldots \mathbf{R}_m)_n = f_n (r_1, r_2, \ldots r_m)$; where the latter is equal to:

$$\frac{(\mathbf{R}_1)_n}{(r_1 - r_2)(r_1 - r_3) \ldots (r_1 - r_m)} + \frac{(\mathbf{R}_2)_n}{(r_2 - r_1)(r_2 - r_3) \ldots (r_2 - r_m)}$$

$$+ \ldots + \frac{(\mathbf{R}_m)_n}{(r_m - r_1)(r_m - r_2) \ldots (r_m - r_{m-1})}$$

This is the formula as long as all the r's are unequal.[1]

We will first show that:

$$(r_1 - r_2) f_n (r_1, r_2, r_3, \ldots r_m)$$
$$= f_n (r_1, r_3, \ldots r_m) - f_n (r_2, r_3, \ldots r_m) \qquad (1)$$

The coefficients of $(\mathbf{R}_1)_n$ and $(\mathbf{R}_2)_n$ on the right hand side of (1) are plainly:

(a) $\dfrac{1}{(r_1 - r_3) \ldots (r_1 - r_m)} = \dfrac{(r_1 - r_2)}{(r_1 - r_2)(r_1 - r_3) \ldots (r_1 - r_m)}$

(b) $\dfrac{-1}{(r_2 - r_3) \ldots (r_2 - r_m)} = \dfrac{(r_1 - r_2)}{(r_2 - r_1)(r_2 - r_3) \ldots (r_2 - r_m)}$

The coefficient of $(\mathbf{R}_3)_n$ (and similarly for other terms) is as follows:

$$\frac{1}{(r_3 - r_4)(r_3 - r_5) \ldots (r_3 - r_m)} \left[\frac{1}{(r_3 - r_1)} - \frac{1}{(r_3 - r_2)} \right]$$
$$= \frac{(r_1 - r_2)}{(r_3 - r_1)(r_3 - r_2)(r_3 - r_4) \ldots (r_3 - r_m)}$$

Thus the identity in (1) is proved. It follows from this identity that, since $f_0(r_1) = 1$,

$$f_0(r_1, r_2) \quad = 0$$
$$f_0(r_1, r_2, r_3) = 0 \text{ etc.}$$

Therefore $f_n(r_1, \ldots r_m)$ and $(\mathbf{R}_1 \ldots \mathbf{R}_m)_n$ are identical:

(a) for $n = 0$ and any m.
(b) for $m = 1$ and any n.

Now $(\mathbf{R}_1 \ldots \mathbf{R}_m)_{n+1}$

$$= \sum_1^{n+1} (\mathbf{R}_1 \ldots \mathbf{R}_{m-1})_{t-1} (1 + r_m)^{n+1-t}$$

$$= (\mathbf{R}_1 \ldots \mathbf{R}_{m-1})_n + \sum_1^n (\mathbf{R}_1 \ldots \mathbf{R}_{m-1})_{t-1} (1 + r_m)^{n+1-t}$$

$$= (\mathbf{R}_1 \ldots \mathbf{R}_{m-1})_n + (1 + r_m) \sum_1^n (\mathbf{R}_1 \ldots \mathbf{R}_{m-1})_{t-1} (1 + r_m)^{n-t}$$

$$= (\mathbf{R}_1 \ldots \mathbf{R}_{m-1})_n + (1 + r_m) (\mathbf{R}_1 \ldots \mathbf{R}_m)_n \qquad (2)$$

---

[1] In the special case when $r = r_1 = r_2 = \ldots = r_m$,
$$f_n = \frac{n (n - 1) \ldots (n - m + 2)}{(m - 1)!} (1 + r)^{n-m+1}$$

38

Furthermore:

$$f_{n+1}(r_1, \ldots r_m) - (1 + r_m) f_n(r_1, \ldots r_m)$$

$$= \frac{(\mathbf{R}_1)_n (r_1 - r_m)}{(r_1 - r_2) \ldots (r_1 - r_m)} + \ldots + \frac{(\mathbf{R}_{m-1})_n (r_{m-1} - r_m)}{(r_{m-1} - r_1) \ldots (r_{m-1} - r_m)}$$

$$= f_n(r_1, \ldots r_{m-1}) \tag{3}$$

This is the same as equation (2). Thus for any value of n and m both the formula for $f_n(r_1, \ldots r_m)$ and $(\mathbf{R}_1 \ldots \mathbf{R}_m)_n$ can be deduced from the same basic values for $n = 0$ and $m = 1$ by the same rules. They are therefore identical.

c.   Some useful identities

Now we have proved the identity in (b) above, it follows from equation (1) that:

$$(r_1 - r_2)\, \mathbf{R}_1\mathbf{R}_2 \quad = \mathbf{R}_1 - \mathbf{R}_2$$
$$(r_1 - r_2)\, \mathbf{R}_1\mathbf{R}_2\mathbf{R}_3 = \mathbf{R}_1\mathbf{R}_3 - \mathbf{R}_2\mathbf{R}_3$$

A particular case of the latter can be deduced when $r_2 = 0$. If $r_1 = j$ and $r_3 = r$, a relation used in the text is:

$j\mathbf{ROJ} = \mathbf{RJ} - \mathbf{RO}$

In fact, if a period (.) is used as an operating symbol such that, for example:

$\mathbf{R}_1\mathbf{R}_2 \,.\, \mathbf{R}_3\mathbf{R}_4 = \mathbf{R}_1\mathbf{R}_2\mathbf{R}_3\mathbf{R}_4$

Then $\mathbf{R}_1\mathbf{R}_2$ may always be replaced by $\dfrac{\mathbf{R}_1 - \mathbf{R}_2}{r_1 - r_2}$ and normal distributive rules apply. For example:

$$\mathbf{R}_1\mathbf{R}_2\mathbf{R}_3\mathbf{R}_4 = \mathbf{R}_1\mathbf{R}_2 \,.\, \mathbf{R}_3\mathbf{R}_4 = \frac{(\mathbf{R}_1 - \mathbf{R}_2)}{(r_1 - r_2)} \cdot \frac{(\mathbf{R}_3 - \mathbf{R}_4)}{(r_3 - r_4)}$$

$$= \frac{1}{(r_1 - r_2)(r_3 - r_4)} (\mathbf{R}_1\mathbf{R}_3 - \mathbf{R}_2\mathbf{R}_3 - \mathbf{R}_1\mathbf{R}_4 + \mathbf{R}_2\mathbf{R}_4)$$

d.   Initial values

We shall prove by induction that:

$$f_n(r_1 \ldots r_m) = 0 \qquad \text{for } n < m - 1 \tag{4}$$
$$= 1 \qquad \text{for } n = m - 1 \tag{5}$$
$$= m + \sum_1^m r_s \text{ for } n = m \tag{6}$$

If these equations are true for m, we shall show that they are true for $(m + 1)$. Using equation (1):

$$(r_1 - r_2) f_n (r_1, r_2 \ldots r_{m+1}) = f_n(r_1, r_3 \ldots r_{m+1}) - f_n (r_2, r_3 \ldots r_{m+1})$$
$$= 0 - 0 \quad \text{for } n < m - 1$$
$$= 1 - 1 \quad \text{for } n = m - 1$$
$$= r_1 - r_2 \text{ for } n = m$$

Hence equations (4) and (5) are true for $(m + 1)$. Now using equation (3):

$$f_{m+1}(r_1, \ldots r_{m+1}) = (1 + r_{m+1}) f_m(r_1 \ldots r_{m+1}) + f_m(r_1 \ldots r_m)$$
$$= 1 + r_{m+1} + m + \sum_1^m r_s$$
$$= (m + 1) + \sum_1^{m+1} r_s$$

Therefore equation (6) is true for $(m + 1)$.

e. Difference equation

Define the increment in the function from n to $n + 1$ as follows:

$$\Delta (\mathbf{R}_1 \mathbf{R}_2 \ldots \mathbf{R}_m)_n = (\mathbf{R}_1 \mathbf{R}_2 \ldots \mathbf{R}_m)_{n+1} - (\mathbf{R}_1 \mathbf{R}_2 \ldots \mathbf{R}_m)_n$$

Then it follows from equation (2) in (b) above that:

$$\Delta (\mathbf{R}_1 \mathbf{R}_2 \ldots \mathbf{R}_m)_n - r_m(\mathbf{R}_1 \mathbf{R}_2 \ldots \mathbf{R}_m)_n = (\mathbf{R}_1 \mathbf{R}_2 \ldots \mathbf{R}_{m-1})_n$$

Hence if $\Delta Z_n - r_m Z_n = a(\mathbf{R}_1 \mathbf{R}_2 \ldots \mathbf{R}_{m-1})_n$

$$Z_n = Z_0(\mathbf{R}_m)_n + a(\mathbf{R}_1 \mathbf{R}_2 \ldots \mathbf{R}_m)_n$$

ANNEX 2

TARGET RATE OF GROWTH

Gross Domestic Product

The problem is to determine F, if $V = V_0\mathbf{R}$.
As initial assumptions:

$$
\begin{array}{ll}
\text{GDP} & (V_0) = 1 \\
\text{Debt} & (D_0) = 0 \\
\text{Savings} & (S_0) = s_0 = kj_0
\end{array}
$$

We shall define h as follows:

$$h = qi$$

Then the expressions for F and D are:

$$\frac{F}{k} = (r - j)\Delta(\mathbf{RH}) + (j - j_0)\mathbf{H}$$

$$\frac{D}{k} = (r - j)\mathbf{RH} + (j - j_0)\mathbf{OH}$$

For, given F:

$$V = 1 + j_0\mathbf{OJ} + (r - j)\,[\Delta(\mathbf{RHJ}) - qi\mathbf{RHJ}]$$
$$+ (j - j_0)\,[\mathbf{HJ} - qi\mathbf{OHJ}]$$

41

Since $qi = h$ and (from Annex 1c and 1e):

$$\Delta(\mathbf{RHJ}) - h\mathbf{RHJ} = \mathbf{RJ}$$
$$\mathbf{HJ} - h\mathbf{OHJ} = \mathbf{OJ}$$
$$V = 1 + j_0\mathbf{OJ} + (r - j)\mathbf{RJ} + (j - j_0)\mathbf{OJ}$$
$$= \mathbf{R}$$

Gross National Product

If the target rate of growth is applicable to GNP, so that $Z = Z_0\mathbf{R}$ and $Z_0 = V_0 = 1$, the expression for F is:

$$\frac{F(1 - ki)}{k} = (r - j)\,\Delta(\mathbf{RH'}) + (j - j_0)\mathbf{H'}$$

Where $h' = \dfrac{(q - s)i}{1 - ki}$

And $\dfrac{D(1 - ki)}{k} = (r - j)\mathbf{RH'} + (j - j_0)\mathbf{OH'}$

For given F,

$$Z = 1 + j_0\mathbf{OJ} + \frac{(r - j)}{1 - ki}\,[\Delta(\mathbf{RH'J}) - qi\mathbf{RH'J} - ki\mathbf{RH'}]$$

$$+ \frac{j - j_0}{1 - ki}\,[\mathbf{H'J} - qi\mathbf{OH'J} - ki\mathbf{OH'}]$$

For, substituting for qi in the first expression in brackets:

$$\Delta(\mathbf{RH'J}) - [h'(1 - ki) + is)]\,\mathbf{RH'J} - ki\mathbf{RH'}$$
$$= \mathbf{RJ} + ki(h' - j)\,\mathbf{RH'J} - ki\mathbf{RH'}$$
$$= \mathbf{RJ} + ki(\mathbf{RH'} - \mathbf{RJ}) - ki\mathbf{RH'}$$
$$= \mathbf{RJ}\,(1 - ki)$$

The second expression in brackets simplifies in the same way to:

$$\mathbf{OJ}\,(1 - ki)$$

And: $\quad Z = 1 + j_0\mathbf{OJ} + (r - j)\mathbf{RJ} + (j - j_0)\mathbf{OJ}$
$\qquad\qquad = \mathbf{R}$

In the first of these two examples, debt will become insupportable, if GNP becomes negative. GNP equals:

$$\mathbf{R} - iD$$
$$= \mathbf{R} - ki(r - j)\mathbf{RH} - ki(j - j_0)\mathbf{OH}$$

If r exceeds h, GNP will become negative, if:

$$ki(r - j) > r - h$$
i.e. $\quad h - is > r(1 - ki)$
i.e. $\quad h' > r$

If h exceeds r, GNP will become negative, if:

$$\frac{j - j_0}{h} > \frac{j - r}{h - r}$$

i.e. $\qquad > \dfrac{(j - j_0) - (r - j_0)}{h - r}$

i.e. $\quad \dfrac{j - j_0}{h} < \dfrac{r - j_0}{r}$

$$\frac{h}{r} > \frac{j - j_0}{r - j_0}$$

Hence debt becomes insupportable within the range:

$$h' > r > \frac{j_0 h}{h - j + j_0}$$

In the second case when $\text{GNP} = \mathbf{R}$, it is obvious that GNP cannot, by definition, become negative. But debt can grow faster than GNP. The condition for this can be proved similarly to be:

$$h' > r > \frac{j_0 h'}{h' - j + j_0}$$

In both cases, it is a necessary (but not sufficient) condition for debt to be insupportable that $h > j$, from which it can be shown that

$$h' > h > j.$$

ANNEX 3

INVESTMENT WITH A TWO-YEAR LAG

In this annex we shall develop an expression for GNP, when the income resulting from an investment starts not in the year following the investment, but in the subsequent year. In other words, there is a two-year lag. It will be assumed that there is zero interest.

Let us first consider an economy without external aid and with a constant savings rate. Previously, with a one-year lag, we had a relationship such that:

$$k\Delta Z_n = I_n = sZ_n$$

or

$$\Delta Z_n = jZ_n$$

But now it is the increment in income from year $(n + 1)$ to $(n + 2)$ which depends on savings in year n. Therefore:

$$\Delta Z_{n+1} = jZ_n$$

The solution to this is of the form:

$$Z_n = A\mathbf{U}_n$$

where

$$u(1 + u) = j$$

This equation has two roots, which we shall call u' and u''. One of them, say, u', is slightly less than j. The other, u'', is related to u' in the following ways:

$$u' + u'' = -1$$
$$u'\, u'' = -j$$

The full expression for Z_n thus includes both u' and u'' and is of the form:

$$Z_n = A'\mathbf{U}'_n + A''\mathbf{U}''_n$$

The constants, A' and A'', depend on both Z_0 and Z_1 because of the lagged relationship between investment and income. Specifically, it can be shown that:

$$Z_n = Z_1\mathbf{U}'\mathbf{U}''_n + Z_0 j\mathbf{U}'\mathbf{U}''_{n-1}$$

Now $(1 + u'') = u'$ which is small, so that, for any but the smallest values of n, $\mathbf{U}''_n$ is negligible. Hence, for values of n over 5 (say), we can approximate as follows:

$$Z_n = \frac{Z_1\mathbf{U}'_n}{u' - u''} + \frac{Z_0 j\mathbf{U}'_{n-1}}{u' - u''}$$
$$= \frac{\mathbf{U}'_n}{1 + 2u'}[Z_1 + Z_0 u']$$

This means that the economy tends to grow at a rate u'. If, in fact, we assume that $Z_1 = (1 + u')Z_0$, then we can simplify still further and say that:

$$Z_n = Z_0\mathbf{U}'_n$$

The effect, then, is to reduce the rate of growth a little. With a three-year lag, it would be reduced a little more. The corresponding values of j and u' in a few cases would be:

u'	j	
	2-year lag	3-year lag
.04	.0416	.0433
.05	.0525	.0551
.06	.0636	.0674

The lag, in sum, increases the effective capital-output ratio. Whether it is, in practice, worth observing the relationship between investment and income with a lag and then adjusting for it is seriously open to question.

External assistance complicates the problem considerably. If there is external assistance in year t of $ka\mathbf{R}_t$, the income from this investment will be $a\mathbf{R}_t$ in year $(t + 2)$. In the subsequent $n - (t + 2)$ years (i.e. up to and including year n), this will grow to:

$$Z = a\mathbf{R}_t\, \mathbf{U}'\mathbf{U}''_{n-t-1}$$

As a result of the series of investments $ka\mathbf{R}_t$ from $t = 0$ to $t = n - 2$, income will equal:

$$Z_n = \sum_{t=0}^{n-2} a\mathbf{R}_t\, \mathbf{U}'\mathbf{U}''_{n-t-1}$$

$$= \sum_{t=1}^{n-1} a\mathbf{R}_{t-1}\, \mathbf{U}'\mathbf{U}''_{n-t}$$

When $t = n$, $\mathbf{U}'\mathbf{U}''_{n-t} = \mathbf{U}'\mathbf{U}''_0 = 0$, therefore:

$$Z = \sum_{t=1}^{n} a\mathbf{R}_{t-1}\, \mathbf{U}'\mathbf{U}''_{n-t}$$

$$= a\mathbf{U}'\mathbf{U}''\mathbf{R}_n$$

Again this can be approximated by omitting $\mathbf{U}''_n$:

$$Z_n = a\left[\frac{\mathbf{U}'_n}{(u' - r)(u' - u'')} + \frac{\mathbf{R}_n}{(r - u')(r - u'')}\right]$$

$$= \frac{a}{(u' - r)}\left[\frac{\mathbf{U}'_n}{(1 + 2u')} - \frac{\mathbf{R}_n}{(1 + u' + r)}\right]$$

The full expression for Z_n can be obtained by combining the two parts:

$$Z_n = Z_1\mathbf{U}'\mathbf{U}''_n + Z_0\,j\mathbf{U}'\mathbf{U}''_{n-1} + a\mathbf{U}'\mathbf{U}''\mathbf{R}_n$$

ANNEX 4

NOTATION, BREVITY, AND ACCURACY

In the first part of a study by Qayum[1] of the effects of a single loan on savings and income, it is assumed that the loan is repaid in equal annual installments without a grace period and interest is' paid on the outstanding balance. The savings function is implicitly assumed to be on a domestic savings basis. A calculation of the aggregate savings over the life of the loan is made in order to see whether this aggregate is positive or negative. Since aggregate savings determine the income ascribable to the loan in the year following the final installment on it, this is the same as asking whether income in that year is positive or negative.

This question can be answered fairly simply. From Table 2 (page 25), we know that the *indirect* addition to GNP from a single investment of ka in year $(n + 1)$ is:

$$a(j - i)\mathbf{OJ}$$

However, repayment of the loan in equal annual installments over a period of n years means that there is a corresponding series

---

[1] A. Qayum, "Long Term Economic Criteria for Foreign Loans," *The Economic Journal*, LXXVI, No. 302, (June 1966).

of negative investments, each of $\frac{ka}{n}$. Each of these yields a terminal *indirect* addition to income in year $(n + 1)$. When added together, they equal:

$$-\frac{a}{n}(j - i)\mathbf{OOJ}$$

Since the loan is repaid, the total external investment is zero and the *direct* additions cancel out. The net effect on income is therefore:

$$Z_{n+1} = a(j - i)\left(\mathbf{OJ} - \frac{\mathbf{OOJ}}{n}\right)$$
$$= \frac{a(j - i)}{j}\left(\mathbf{J} - \frac{\mathbf{OJ}}{n}\right)$$

The second of these expressions is necessarily positive since $\mathbf{OJ}_n$ is the sum of $\mathbf{J}_t$ from $t = 0$ to $n - 1$. The sign of Z_{n+1}, therefore, turns on whether j is greater or less than i. The period of repayment is irrelevant.

Qayum does not give a complete expression for the aggregate savings. He states the savings in each year are as follows (the symbols have been changed to conform to usage here):

$$S_t = ka\left[j - \left(1 - \frac{t - 1}{n}\right)i - \frac{1}{t}\right]$$

Aggregate savings are then expressed as follows:

$$S^* = ka + \sum_{t=1}^{n} \frac{S_t(1 - j^{n-t+1})}{1 - j}$$

This is not only far more complicated. It is also quite incorrect. This statement is not made in a spirit of triumphant discovery of error; the writer has discovered too many similar ones of his own for that. The moral is, rather, that a simplified notational system can make life easier for both writer and reader.

The error which Qayum makes is as follows. He states that the savings S_t in year t lead to additional savings in year $(t + 1)$ of jS_t and in year $(t + 2)$ of $j^2 S_t$ and so on. The first part of this is correct. The income in year $(t + 1)$ is $\frac{S_t}{k}$ and savings are jS_t. But

48

income in year $(t + 2)$ will be $\frac{S_t}{k}(1 + j)$ and savings correspondingly $jS_t(1 + j)$ and *not* j^2S_t. These savings, which may be positive or negative, are greatly understated.

Somewhat the same error appears to have been made in Little and Clifford, *op. cit.*, p. 104 (American edition), where the "multiplier" effect of savings is described. The multiplier is, in effect, $\frac{1}{(1 - j)}$, the same as Qayum's. Again, this does not take into account that income from an investment continues *each year* and the income from the invested savings does the same.

It is true, of course, that, as pointed out at the beginning of Chapter III, we have made the unsatisfactory assumption that income continues indefinitely. But the error is not nearly so great and, if the investments have longer lives than the time-horizon being considered, is not an error at all.

It can be quantified. If income from a single investment stops after m years, the effect is the same as a negative investment (without interest). The expression in Table 2 for GDP in year $n + 1$, provided that n is greater than m, will be:

$$a\mathbf{J}_n - qai\mathbf{OJ}_n - a\mathbf{J}_{n-m}$$

The condition for this becoming negative can be deduced from the coefficient of $a\mathbf{J}_n$ and will now be:

$$1 - \mathbf{J}_{-m} < \frac{qi}{j}$$

For very short-term investments with high capital-output ratios, it is possible that this can become negative, even on a national savings basis.

ACCUMULATION FUNCTION TABLE 1:   Second Generation, 5 Years. $IJ_5 =$

Interest rate (percent)

Growth rate (percent)	0	1	2	3	4	5	6	7	8	9	10
0	5.000	5.101	5.204	5.309	5.416	5.526	5.637	5.751	5.867	5.98	6.11
1	5.101	5.203	5.307	5.413	5.521	5.632	5.744	5.859	5.976	6.10	6.22
2	5.204	5.307	5.412	5.519	5.629	5.740	5.854	5.969	6.087	6.21	6.33
3	5.309	5.413	5.519	5.628	5.738	5.850	5.965	6.082	6.201	6.32	6.45
4	5.416	5.521	5.629	5.738	5.849	5.963	6.079	6.197	6.317	6.44	6.56
5	5.526	5.632	5.740	5.850	5.963	6.078	6.194	6.314	6.435	6.56	6.68
6	5.637	5.744	5.854	5.965	6.079	6.194	6.312	6.433	6.555	6.68	6.81
7	5.751	5.859	5.969	6.082	6.197	6.314	6.433	6.554	6.678	6.80	6.93
8	5.867	5.976	6.087	6.201	6.317	6.435	6.555	6.678	6.802	6.93	7.06
9	5.985	6.095	6.208	6.322	6.439	6.559	6.680	6.804	6.930	7.06	7.19
10	6.105	6.217	6.330	6.446	6.564	6.685	6.807	6.932	7.059	7.19	7.32
11	6.228	6.340	6.455	6.572	6.692	6.813	6.937	7.063	7.191	7.32	7.45
12	6.353	6.467	6.583	6.701	6.821	6.944	7.069	7.196	7.325	7.46	7.59
13	6.480	6.595	6.712	6.832	6.953	7.077	7.203	7.331	7.462	7.60	7.73
14	6.610	6.726	6.844	6.965	7.088	7.213	7.340	7.469	7.601	7.74	7.87
15	6.742	6.860	6.979	7.101	7.225	7.351	7.479	7.610	7.743	7.88	8.02
20	7.442	7.565	7.690	7.818	7.948	8.080	8.215	8.352	8.492	8.63	8.78
25	8.207	8.336	8.468	8.602	8.739	8.877	9.019	9.162	9.308	9.46	9.61

50

ACCUMULATION FUNCTION TABLE 2:   Second Generation, 10 Years. $IJ_{10} =$

Interest rate (*percent*)

Growth rate (*percent*)	0	1	2	3	4	5	6	7	8	9	10
0	10.000	10.462	10.950	11.464	12.006	12.578	13.181	13.816	14.487	15.19	15.94
1	10.462	10.937	11.437	11.965	12.521	13.107	13.725	14.375	15.061	15.78	16.55
2	10.950	11.437	11.951	12.492	13.062	13.663	14.296	14.963	15.666	16.41	17.18
3	11.464	11.965	12.492	13.048	13.633	14.249	14.898	15.581	16.300	17.06	17.85
4	12.006	12.521	13.062	13.633	14.233	14.865	15.530	16.230	16.967	17.74	18.56
5	12.578	13.107	13.663	14.249	14.865	15.513	16.195	16.913	17.668	18.46	19.30
6	13.181	13.725	14.296	14.898	15.530	16.195	16.895	17.630	18.404	19.22	20.07
7	13.816	14.375	14.963	15.581	16.230	16.913	17.630	18.385	19.177	20.01	20.89
8	14.487	15.061	15.666	16.300	16.967	17.668	18.404	19.177	19.990	20.84	21.74
9	15.193	15.784	16.405	17.057	17.742	18.462	19.217	20.011	20.844	21.72	22.64
10	15.937	16.546	17.184	17.855	18.558	19.297	20.072	20.886	21.741	22.64	23.58
11	16.722	17.348	18.005	18.694	19.417	20.175	20.971	21.807	22.683	23.60	24.57
12	17.549	18.193	18.869	19.577	20.320	21.099	21.917	22.774	23.673	24.62	25.61
13	18.420	19.083	19.778	20.507	21.270	22.071	22.910	23.790	24.713	25.68	26.69
14	19.337	20.020	20.735	21.485	22.270	23.093	23.955	24.858	25.805	26.80	27.84
15	20.304	21.007	21.743	22.514	23.321	24.167	25.052	25.980	26.952	27.97	29.04
20	25.959	26.774	27.626	28.517	29.447	30.419	31.435	32.497	33.607	34.77	35.98
25	33.253	34.203	35.192	36.224	37.300	38.422	39.591	40.812	42.084	43.41	44.80

51

ACCUMULATION FUNCTION TABLE 3:   Second Generation, 15 Years. $IJ_{15} =$

Growth rate (percent)	Interest rate (percent)										
	0	1	2	3	4	5	6	7	8	9	10
0	15.000	16.097	17.293	18.599	20.024	21.579	23.276	25.129	27.152	29.36	31.77
1	16.097	17.242	18.490	19.850	21.332	22.949	24.712	26.634	28.731	31.02	33.51
2	17.293	18.490	19.792	21.210	22.754	24.435	26.267	28.263	30.438	32.81	35.39
3	18.599	19.850	21.210	22.689	24.298	26.048	27.953	30.027	32.284	34.74	37.42
4	20.024	21.332	22.754	24.298	25.975	27.798	29.781	31.936	34.281	36.83	39.61
5	21.579	22.949	24.435	26.048	27.798	29.699	31.763	34.005	36.441	39.09	41.97
6	23.276	24.712	26.267	27.953	29.781	31.763	33.914	36.247	38.781	41.53	44.52
7	25.129	26.634	28.263	30.027	31.936	34.005	36.247	38.678	41.314	44.17	47.27
8	27.152	28.731	30.438	32.284	34.281	36.441	38.781	41.314	44.058	47.03	50.25
9	29.361	31.019	32.809	34.742	36.831	39.089	41.531	44.173	47.031	50.13	53.48
10	31.772	33.514	35.392	37.418	39.605	41.966	44.517	47.274	50.254	53.48	56.96
11	34.405	36.236	38.208	40.333	42.624	45.094	47.761	50.639	53.747	57.11	60.73
12	37.280	39.205	41.277	43.507	45.908	48.495	51.283	54.291	57.535	61.04	64.82
13	40.417	42.444	44.622	46.963	49.481	52.192	55.110	58.254	61.642	65.29	69.23
14	43.842	45.977	48.267	50.727	53.370	56.211	59.267	62.556	66.096	69.91	74.02
15	47.580	49.829	52.240	54.826	57.601	60.581	63.783	67.225	70.927	74.91	79.20
20	72.035	74.979	78.118	81.465	85.038	88.854	92.932	97.292	101.957	106.95	112.30
25	109.687	113.586	117.721	122.108	126.766	131.714	136.974	142.570	148.527	154.87	161.63

ACCUMULATION FUNCTION TABLE 4: Second Generation, 20 Years. II_{20} =

Interest rate (*percent*)

Growth rate (*percent*)	0	1	2	3	4	5	6	7	8	9	10
0	20.000	22.019	24.297	26.870	29.778	33.066	36.786	40.995	45.762	51.16	57.27
1	22.019	24.162	26.576	29.296	32.364	35.828	39.739	44.158	49.154	54.80	61.19
2	24.297	26.576	29.136	32.016	35.259	38.912	43.030	47.675	52.917	58.84	65.52
3	26.870	29.296	32.016	35.070	38.501	42.359	46.701	51.589	57.097	63.30	70.31
4	29.778	32.364	35.259	38.501	42.137	46.217	50.801	55.952	61.746	68.27	75.61
5	33.066	35.828	38.912	42.359	46.217	50.539	55.384	60.819	66.922	73.78	81.48
6	36.786	39.739	43.030	46.701	50.801	55.384	60.512	66.255	72.691	79.91	88.01
7	40.995	44.158	47.675	51.589	55.952	60.819	66.255	72.331	79.127	86.74	95.26
8	45.762	49.154	52.917	57.097	61.746	66.922	72.691	79.127	86.314	94.35	103.33
9	51.160	54.803	58.835	63.305	68.266	73.778	79.909	86.736	94.345	102.83	112.31
10	57.275	61.192	65.519	70.306	75.606	81.484	88.009	95.260	103.327	112.31	122.32
11	64.203	68.421	73.071	78.203	83.874	90.150	97.104	104.816	113.378	122.90	133.48
12	72.052	76.601	81.603	87.113	93.190	99.900	107.319	115.532	124.633	134.73	145.94
13	80.947	85.857	91.247	97.170	103.688	110.872	118.799	127.557	137.243	147.97	159.85
14	91.025	96.333	102.146	108.522	115.524	123.224	131.704	141.054	151.375	162.78	175.40
15	102.444	108.188	114.466	121.337	128.867	137.132	146.216	156.211	167.223	179.37	192.78
20	186.688	195.355	204.731	214.891	225.915	237.895	250.932	265.138	280.639	297.57	316.10
25	342.945	356.317	370.653	386.046	402.595	420.414	439.627	460.369	482.795	507.07	533.39

ACCUMULATION FUNCTION TABLE 5: Second Generation, 25 Years. $IJ_{25} =$

Interest rate (percent)

Growth rate (percent)	0	1	2	3	4	5	6	7	8	9	10
0	25.000	28.243	32.030	36.459	41.646	47.727	54.864	63.249	73.106	84.70	98.35
1	28.243	31.743	35.817	40.567	46.113	52.598	60.189	69.083	79.515	91.76	106.14
2	32.030	35.817	40.211	45.317	51.262	58.192	66.282	75.737	86.798	99.75	114.93
3	36.459	40.567	45.317	50.820	57.206	64.629	73.270	83.341	95.094	108.82	124.87
4	41.646	46.113	51.262	57.206	64.083	72.052	81.302	92.053	104.566	119.14	136.15
5	47.727	52.598	58.192	64.629	72.052	80.627	90.551	102.054	115.404	130.92	148.97
6	54.864	60.189	66.282	73.270	81.302	90.551	101.223	113.556	127.830	144.37	163.57
7	63.249	69.083	75.737	83.341	92.053	102.054	113.556	126.809	142.104	159.78	180.24
8	73.106	79.515	86.798	95.094	104.566	115.404	127.830	142.104	158.529	177.46	199.31
9	84.701	91.758	99.750	108.822	119.145	130.918	144.374	159.782	177.460	197.78	221.16
10	98.347	106.136	114.926	124.870	136.148	148.967	163.571	180.242	199.311	221.16	246.24
11	114.413	123.030	132.721	143.646	155.995	169.985	185.872	203.951	224.566	248.12	275.08
12	133.334	142.888	153.595	165.625	179.178	194.481	211.803	231.453	253.790	279.23	308.27
13	155.620	166.234	178.090	191.368	206.274	223.052	241.981	263.385	287.641	315.19	346.53
14	181.871	193.688	206.844	221.528	237.961	256.395	277.125	300.492	326.891	356.78	390.68
15	212.793	225.975	240.603	256.876	275.028	295.326	318.079	343.644	372.435	404.93	441.68
20	471.981	495.336	520.864	548.838	579.565	613.399	650.745	692.067	737.898	788.85	845.61
25	1,054.791	1,097.564	1,143.727	1,193.655	1,247.771	1,306.557	1,370.557	1,440.391	1,516.761	1,600.47	1,692.42

ACCUMULATION FUNCTION TABLE 6: Third Generation—Zero Growth Rate, 5 Years. $IOJ_5 =$

Interest rate (*percent*)

Growth rate (*percent*)	0	1	2	3	4	5	6	7	8	9	10
0	10.000	10.100	10.202	10.304	10.408	10.513	10.618	10.725	10.833	10.94	11.05
1	10.100	10.202	10.304	10.407	10.511	10.616	10.722	10.829	10.937	11.05	11.16
2	10.202	10.304	10.406	10.509	10.614	10.720	10.826	10.934	11.043	11.15	11.26
3	10.304	10.407	10.509	10.614	10.719	10.825	10.932	11.040	11.149	11.26	11.37
4	10.408	10.511	10.614	10.719	10.824	10.931	11.038	11.147	11.257	11.37	11.48
5	10.513	10.616	10.720	10.825	10.931	11.038	11.146	11.255	11.366	11.48	11.59
6	10.618	10.722	10.826	10.932	11.038	11.146	11.255	11.365	11.475	11.59	11.70
7	10.725	10.829	10.934	11.040	11.147	11.255	11.365	11.475	11.586	11.70	11.81
8	10.833	10.937	11.043	11.149	11.257	11.366	11.475	11.586	11.698	11.81	11.92
9	10.941	11.046	11.152	11.260	11.368	11.477	11.587	11.699	11.811	11.92	12.04
10	11.051	11.157	11.263	11.371	11.480	11.589	11.700	11.812	11.925	12.04	12.15
11	11.162	11.268	11.375	11.483	11.593	11.703	11.814	11.927	12.040	12.15	12.27
12	11.274	11.380	11.488	11.597	11.707	11.817	11.929	12.042	12.156	12.27	12.39
13	11.387	11.494	11.602	11.711	11.822	11.933	12.045	12.159	12.273	12.39	12.51
14	11.501	11.609	11.717	11.827	11.938	12.050	12.163	12.277	12.392	12.51	12.63
15	11.616	11.724	11.833	11.944	12.055	12.167	12.281	12.396	12.511	12.63	12.75
20	12.208	12.319	12.431	12.544	12.658	12.773	12.889	13.007	13.125	13.24	13.36
25	12.828	12.942	13.056	13.172	13.289	13.407	13.526	13.646	13.767	13.89	14.01

ACCUMULATION FUNCTION TABLE 7: Third Generation—Zero Growth Rate, 10 Years. **IOJ**$_{10}$ =

Interest rate (*percent*)

Growth rate (*percent*)	0	1	2	3	4	5	6	7	8	9	10
0	45.000	46.219	47.486	48.796	50.153	51.558	53.013	54.521	56.082	57.70	59.37
1	46.219	47.466	48.752	50.084	51.464	52.892	54.372	55.904	57.491	59.13	60.84
2	47.486	48.752	50.060	51.415	52.819	54.273	55.777	57.335	58.947	60.62	62.35
3	48.796	50.084	51.415	52.795	54.223	55.701	57.231	58.814	60.454	62.15	63.91
4	50.153	51.464	52.819	54.223	55.675	57.179	58.734	60.345	62.011	63.74	65.52
5	51.558	52.892	54.272	55.701	57.179	58.708	60.290	61.928	63.622	65.38	67.19
6	53.013	54.372	55.777	57.231	58.734	60.290	61.900	63.566	65.289	67.07	68.92
7	54.521	55.904	57.335	58.814	60.345	61.928	63.566	65.259	67.012	68.82	70.70
8	56.082	57.491	58.947	60.454	62.011	63.622	65.289	67.012	68.794	70.64	72.54
9	57.699	59.134	60.617	62.151	63.736	65.376	67.071	68.824	70.637	72.51	74.45
10	59.374	60.836	62.346	63.908	65.522	67.191	68.916	70.699	72.543	74.45	76.42
11	61.109	62.598	64.137	65.727	67.370	69.069	70.824	72.639	74.515	76.45	78.46
12	62.906	64.423	65.990	67.610	69.283	71.012	72.799	74.646	76.554	78.53	80.57
13	64.767	66.313	67.909	69.559	71.263	73.023	74.842	76.722	78.664	80.67	82.74
14	66.695	68.270	69.896	71.577	73.312	75.104	76.956	78.869	80.846	82.89	85.00
15	68.691	70.297	71.954	73.665	75.433	77.258	79.144	81.091	83.102	85.18	87.33
20	79.793	81.560	83.383	85.264	87.204	89.205	91.271	93.402	95.601	97.87	100.21
25	93.012	94.961	96.970	99.041	101.175	103.375	105.643	107.980	110.390	112.87	115.44

ACCUMULATION FUNCTION TABLE 8: Third Generation—Zero Growth Rate, 15 Years. IOJ_{15} =

Growth rate (percent)	Interest rate (percent)										
	0	1	2	3	4	5	6	7	8	9	10
0	105.000	109.686	114.670	119.963	125.590	131.571	137.933	144.700	151.901	159.57	167.72
1	109.686	114.525	119.654	125.102	130.891	137.042	143.582	150.536	157.932	165.80	174.17
2	114.670	119.654	124.939	130.549	136.509	142.838	149.564	156.712	164.312	172.39	180.99
3	119.963	125.102	130.549	136.331	142.468	148.983	155.902	163.253	171.064	179.37	188.19
4	125.590	130.891	136.509	142.468	148.789	155.498	162.619	170.181	178.213	186.75	195.81
5	131.571	137.042	142.838	148.983	155.498	162.408	169.740	177.523	185.785	194.56	203.88
6	137.933	143.582	149.564	155.902	162.619	169.740	177.293	185.306	193.808	202.83	212.41
7	144.700	150.536	156.712	163.253	170.181	177.523	185.306	193.557	202.309	211.59	221.45
8	151.901	157.932	164.312	171.064	178.213	185.785	193.808	202.309	211.322	220.88	231.02
9	159.566	165.801	172.393	179.367	186.746	194.559	202.832	211.594	220.880	230.72	241.16
10	167.725	174.173	180.988	188.194	195.815	203.878	212.413	221.449	231.018	241.16	251.90
11	176.412	183.085	190.133	197.581	205.454	213.780	222.588	231.909	241.775	252.22	263.29
12	185.664	192.571	199.863	207.565	215.702	224.302	233.396	243.014	253.190	263.96	275.36
13	195.519	202.672	210.219	218.186	226.599	235.486	244.879	254.807	265.307	276.41	288.17
14	206.017	213.427	221.242	229.486	238.188	247.376	257.081	267.334	278.172	289.63	301.75
15	217.203	224.882	232.977	241.513	250.517	260.018	270.049	280.642	291.833	303.66	316.16
20	285.175	294.412	304.120	314.331	325.072	336.377	348.280	360.816	374.025	387.95	402.63
25	378.747	389.958	401.711	414.036	426.968	440.541	454.794	469.766	485.498	502.04	519.43

ACCUMULATION FUNCTION TABLE 9: Third Generation—Zero Growth Rate, 20 Years. $IOJ_{20} =$

Interest rate (percent)

Growth rate (percent)	0	1	2	3	4	5	6	7	8	9	10
0	190.000	201.896	214.868	229.012	244.452	261.319	279.759	299.935	322.024	346.22	372.75
1	201.896	214.321	227.840	242.569	258.637	276.175	295.332	316.275	339.186	364.26	391.73
2	214.868	227.840	241.943	257.299	274.036	292.286	312.205	333.962	357.743	383.75	412.22
3	229.012	242.569	257.299	273.325	290.772	309.780	330.507	353.128	377.832	404.83	434.35
4	244.452	258.637	274.036	290.772	308.973	328.788	350.375	373.914	399.597	427.64	458.28
5	261.319	276.175	292.286	309.780	328.788	349.461	371.962	396.477	423.200	452.35	484.18
6	279.759	295.332	312.205	330.507	350.375	371.962	395.440	420.991	448.819	479.15	512.24
7	299.935	316.275	333.962	353.128	373.914	396.476	420.991	447.644	476.648	508.23	542.65
8	322.024	339.186	357.743	377.832	399.597	423.200	448.819	476.648	506.901	539.81	575.65
9	346.223	364.264	383.753	404.829	427.641	452.354	479.151	508.231	539.814	574.15	611.49
10	372.750	391.734	412.220	434.352	458.282	484.181	512.235	542.650	575.652	611.49	650.43
11	401.844	421.839	443.394	466.656	491.782	518.948	548.345	580.184	614.696	652.14	692.78
12	433.770	454.850	477.551	502.023	528.429	556.950	587.781	621.139	657.262	696.41	738.87
13	468.822	491.065	514.995	540.765	568.542	598.511	630.875	665.856	703.697	744.67	789.06
14	507.321	530.815	556.063	583.223	612.468	643.988	677.992	714.706	754.382	797.30	843.75
15	549.624	574.461	601.125	629.777	660.595	693.776	729.533	768.101	809.737	854.72	903.37
20	833.440	866.679	902.170	940.104	980.687	1,024.147	1,070.731	1,120.711	1,174.383	1,232.07	1,294.13
25	1,291.779	1,337.191	1,385.423	1,436.702	1,491.270	1,549.394	1,611.364	1,677.496	1,748.134	1,823.65	1,904.46

ACCUMULATION FUNCTION TABLE 10: Third Generation—Zero Growth Rate, 25 Years. **IOJ**$_{25}$ =

Interest rate (*percent*)

Growth rate (*percent*)	0	1	2	3	4	5	6	7	8	9	10
0	300.000	324.314	351.514	381.974	416.147	454.542	497.741	546.414	601.324	663.34	733.47
1	324.314	350.021	378.714	410.804	446.758	487.099	532.427	583.431	640.897	705.72	778.93
2	351.514	378.714	409.032	442.894	480.781	523.227	570.855	624.375	684.594	752.44	828.96
3	381.974	410.804	442.894	478.687	518.667	563.393	613.508	669.745	732.934	804.03	884.11
4	416.147	446.758	480.781	518.667	560.917	608.120	660.929	720.104	786.501	861.10	945.02
5	454.542	487.099	523.227	563.393	608.120	658.008	713.739	776.096	845.961	924.34	1,012.40
6	497.741	532.427	570.855	613.508	660.929	713.738	772.647	838.454	912.072	994.55	1,087.06
7	546.414	583.431	624.375	669.745	720.104	776.096	838.454	908.002	985.691	1,072.59	1,169.93
8	601.324	640.897	684.594	732.934	786.501	845.961	912.072	985.691	1,067.795	1,159.49	1,262.06
9	663.343	705.721	752.437	804.027	861.099	924.344	994.546	1,072.592	1,159.493	1,256.40	1,364.62
10	733.470	778.932	828.959	884.111	945.019	1,012.399	1,087.064	1,169.934	1,262.055	1,364.62	1,478.96
11	812.848	861.701	915.367	974.426	1,039.534	1,111.437	1,190.976	1,279.107	1,376.912	1,485.62	1,606.63
12	902.782	955.370	1,013.035	1,076.384	1,146.099	1,222.953	1,307.822	1,401.696	1,505.697	1,621.10	1,749.34
13	1,004.766	1,061.470	1,123.539	1,191.603	1,266.374	1,348.655	1,439.358	1,539.508	1,650.272	1,772.97	1,909.08
14	1,120.505	1,181.751	1,248.671	1,321.923	1,402.249	1,490.485	1,587.578	1,694.596	1,812.747	1,943.40	2,088.09
15	1,251.953	1,318.213	1,390.482	1,469.448	1,555.882	1,650.659	1,754.761	1,869.299	1,995.529	2,134.87	2,288.92
20	2,234.905	2,335.462	2,444.170	2,561.892	2,689.594	2,828.359	2,979.403	3,144.092	3,323.958	3,520.73	3,736.34
25	4,119.165	4,277.283	4,446.786	4,628.781	4,824.501	5,035.320	5,262.772	5,508.567	5,774.619	6,063.06	6,376.29